P9-AFZ-984

APR 0 3 2006
Green Lake Library

NO LONGER PROPERTY OF
SEATTLE PUBLIC LIBRARY

WOLF

WOLF
LEGEND · ENEMY · ICON

Rebecca L. Grambo

Photographs by Daniel J. Cox

FIREFLY BOOKS

A Firefly Book

Published by Firefly Books Ltd. 2005

Text copyright © 2005 Rebecca L. Grambo
All photographs copyright © 2005 Daniel J. Cox
unless otherwise noted

All rights reserved. No part of this publication may be
reproduced, stored in a retrieval system, or transmitted
in any form or by any means, electronic, mechanical,
photocopying, recording or otherwise, without
the prior written permission of the Publisher.

First printing

Publisher Cataloging-in-Publication Data (U.S.)
Grambo, Rebecca L.
Wolf : legend, enemy, icon / Rebecca L.
Grambo ; photographs by Daniel J. Cox.
[176] p. : col. photos. ; cm.
Includes bibliographical references and index.
Summary: An examination of the human-wolf
relationship, through legends, myths and facts.
ISBN 1-55407-044-9
1. Wolves. 2 Human-animal relationships.
I. Cox, Daniel J. II. Title.
599.773 dc22   QL737.C22G736 2005

Library and Archives Canada Cataloguing in Publication
Grambo, Rebecca, 1963-
Wolf : legend, enemy, icon / Rebecca L.
Grambo ; photographs by Daniel J. Cox.
Includes bibliographical references and index.
ISBN 1-55407-044-9
1. Wolves. 2. Human-wolf encounters. 3. Wolves—Folklore.
I. Cox, Daniel J., 1960- II. Title.
QL737.C22G726 2005   599.773   C2005-901181-5

Published in the United States by
Firefly Books (U.S.) Inc.
P.O. Box 1338, Ellicott Station
Buffalo, New York 14205

Published in Canada by
Firefly Books Ltd.
66 Leek Crescent
Richmond Hill, Ontario L4B 1H1

Cover and interior design by Robert Yerks
visualanguage, llc

Printed in Canada by Friesens

*The publisher gratefully
acknowledges the financial support
for our publishing program by the
Canada Council for the Arts and the
Government of Canada through
the Book Publishing Industry
Development Program*

PREVIOUS PAGE The Gundestrup
Cauldron is a silver ritual vessel
found in a Danish bog. Crafted
around the first century B.C., it
portrays the horned Celtic deity
Cernunnos with a wolf on his left
and a stag on his right.

BACK COVER (TOP) Nisga'a Wolf Rattle

BACK COVER (BOTTOM) Gushtasp killing
a wolf, from a miniature painting
from a fifteenth century manuscript
of the epic poem of Shahnama.

ACKNOWLEDGMENTS

For Marlene Kozak —
a wonderful person who adds love, laughter, books and bread to my life.

A project of this size takes the combined efforts and thoughts of many people. My dear friends Dan Cox and Robert Yerks let me run with my ideas, supplying the images and design skills to make them take shape on paper. Michael Worek, Brad Wilson and Charis Cotter at Firefly offered patient support and technical skill in large amounts. Anne Holloway applied her editing expertise. Many people took time to read and comment on portions of the manuscript despite hectic schedules: Paul Paquet, Wolfgang Schleidt, Marilyn Grambo, Glen Grambo, Marlene Kozak, Ric Kessler, and David and Cathryn Miller. Any errors in the book, of course, remain my responsibility. Peter Schleifenbaum at the Haliburton Forest and Wildlife Reserve was kind enough to give me access to his wonderful collection of wolf books and memorabilia. Jody Bissett at the Haliburton Forest Wolf Centre was a great help during my research there. The interlibrary loan staff of the Saskatoon Public Library, especially Louise Carlson at the Rusty McDonald Branch, tracked down some rather esoteric materials in a remarkably short time.

Finally, I must thank everyone, especially my husband, Glen, who put up with the grumpiness of a writer forcing ideas out of her brain and onto paper.

Contents

	Introduction	13
Chapter 1	At the Firelight's Edge	21
Chapter 2	Part of the Pack	39
Chapter 3	Legendary Predator	69
Chapter 4	Warriors and Wolves	93
Chapter 5	Shamans and Shapeshifters	111
Chapter 6	Predator Becomes Prey	125
Chapter 7	At the Edge Again	153
Appendix	Members of the Pack	168
	Notes	170
	Photo Credits	170
	Bibliography	171
	Index	174

INTRODUCTION

I never really liked the story of Little Red Riding Hood. Even as a child, I figured that someone who couldn't tell the difference between her grandmother and a wolf deserved whatever she got. The "big bad wolf" was no more real to me than the giants and ogres of other fairy tales. I didn't make any connection between the storybook villains and the predators that once roamed the South Dakota prairies where I grew up. In fact, I knew so little about real wolves that years ago when I first camped in wolf country, I wondered whether I would recognize the difference between the howling of wolves and of coyotes. Those first howls, unmistakable as they resonated through the woods and within me, were really the beginning of this book.

The animal that most of us think of as "wolf," *Canis lupus*, has been around for about twice as long as Homo sapiens, modern humans. From the moment the two species first encountered each other, the relationship between humans and wolves has shifted and evolved. Wolves through countless generations simply have done what wolves do — hunt and raise families. But the way humans viewed wolves changed as cultural shifts distorted the lens of perception. Legend, enemy and icon — these are the captions we have applied to our image of the wolf.

Early humans shared a nomadic hunting lifestyle with wolves and identified with their social structure and family life. They wrapped wolves in the golden cloth of legend, revering them as creators and helpers. In these early myths, wolves helped to shape the infant Earth, and through their actions brought forth the human race. With great pride, some peo-

Take warning hence, ye children fair;
Of wolves' insidious arts beware;
And as you pass each lonely wood,
Ah! think of small Red-riding-hood.

With custards sent nor loiter slow,
Nor gather blue-bells as ye go;
Get not to bed with grand-mummie,
Lest she a ravenous wolf should be!

—from *Red Riding Hood*, Anonymous. 1801

ples claimed wolves as their direct ancestors. Many cultures told stories of wolves rescuing people in trouble, caring for them and healing their wounds. Used for both curing and harming, wolf magic was extremely strong. Powerful shamans in many cultures drew upon the spirit of the wolf, sometimes even assuming its physical form.

Warriors, too, sought to access the supernatural powers of the animal they saw as a superb predator. From Vikings of the first millennium to late nineteenth-century Pawnee, warriors wore wolfskins and followed rituals designed to merge their essence with that of the wolf. Respect for the wolf remained strong among North America's indigenous peoples, especially the nomadic hunters of the Great Plains, well into recent history.

In other parts of the world, a change in human lifestyle — from hunting to herding — caused many people to hate and fear wolves for the same predatory skills that once appeared admirable. Opportunistic and adaptable, wolves saw domestic flocks as easy prey and farmers came to regard them as the enemy. Another, more insidious, cultural change also took place. With each step toward "civilization," people moved farther away from contact with nature and from the knowledge that humans are part of the natural world, not separate from or above it. They also forgot much of what their ancestors had learned about wolves and wilderness — and what humans don't understand, they often fear.

During the Middle Ages, human imagination merged the images of two threatening beings that lived in the woods — outlaws and wolves — into the idea of the were-wolf. At the same time, the church demonized wolves, making them allegorical symbols of darkness and evil. When Europeans came to the New World, they brought along their livestock and their unfavorable view of wolves. As farmers and ranchers moved west, the war against wolves that began so long ago raged more fiercely than ever. Today, the image of the wolf as a ruthless, lamb-slaughtering enemy still lingers in children's stories, in movies, in advertising campaigns, and in the minds of some people.

But a new view of wolves has also emerged, based in part upon the rediscovery of our interconnection with the natural world. By the last decades of the twentieth century, many people observed the rapidly vanishing wilderness with alarm. The wolf became an icon of the wild, its howl representing a cry for preservation and conservation. Programs to maintain existing wolf populations and to reintroduce animals into areas from which they had been extirpated found solid public support. The restoration of wolves to Yellowstone National Park is a tangible result of this new view. The review process for the Yellowstone project generated a great deal of useful discussion, not just about wolves, but about all wild animals and their needs.

While the current popularity of wolves has expanded our knowledge of them, this knowledge is nearly always remote and two-dimensional, confined to the printed page and illuminated screen. Being in the presence of real wolves is another thing altogether, but not everyone is fortunate enough to have this experience. However, we can explore the thoughts and feelings of people who lived in everyday contact with wolves, thus adding the dimensions of time and space to our existing concept of "wolf." Placing their artifacts and stories alongside information about wolves' natural history and Daniel J. Cox's beautiful images of these magnificent creatures going about their daily lives gives us a chance to hear ancient voices in a new context.

Although we may regard myths and legends as ancient history, for most of the twentieth century stories — both true and false — were the sole source, of information about wolves. Field researchers only began documenting the facts of wolf life about fifty years ago. Until then, we remained much like our early ancestors, crouched by the comforting glow of our fires, telling stories about the beasts that prowled the darkness.

Haida Wolf Mask. Originally had separate ears and was trimmed with hair.

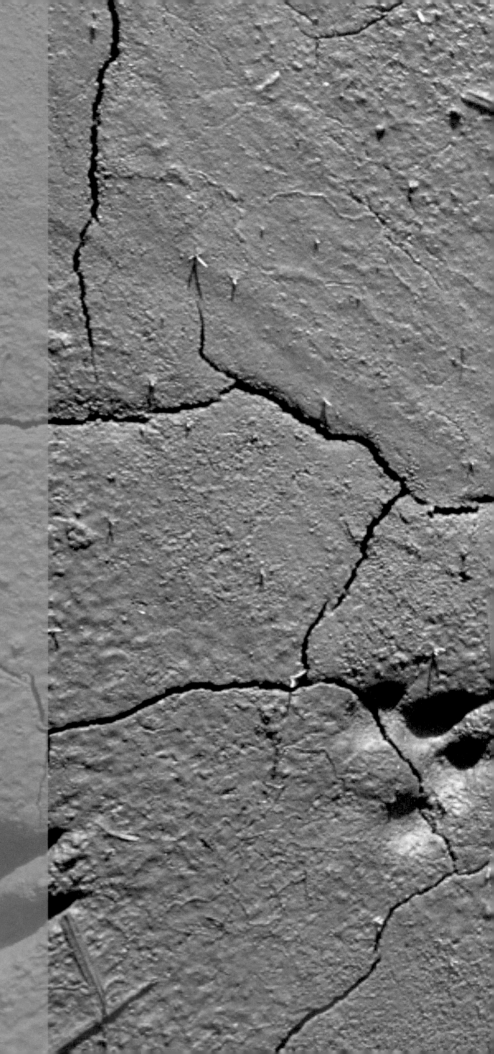

Wolf Helps to Make the World

At the beginning there was nothing but an endless expanse of water. Old Man sat on a log with his four companions: otter, duck, badger and muskrat. He asked the animals, "Do you think there is anything beneath the water? Why don't you dive down and take a look?" The animals slipped into the water and disappeared beneath the surface. Only the muskrat returned, so exhausted that it was barely able to climb back onto the log. It gave Old Man a small ball of mud. Old Man took the mud and began to roll it back and forth in his hands. The mud flattened and grew with amazing speed, eventually forming a platform on which Old Man could stand. Old Man brought forth a wolf and set it free to run across the hardening mud. Wherever the wolf's paws pressed down, a valley appeared. As he traveled farther across the mud plain, mountains rose and water began to flow to make rivers and streams.

—Blackfoot Creation myth

AT THE FIRELIGHT'S EDGE

As far as our memories can reach, and for a misty distance beyond, wolves have played a part in humans' lives and beliefs. Where did they come from and what made them the way they were? Science and natural history offer one kind of answer; myths and legends give another. Paleontologists place the beginnings of the genus Canis — the branch of the Canidae family that contains wolves, coyotes and their relatives — somewhere between seven and ten million years ago, although the gray wolf species appeared only about one million years ago. At one time, wolves roamed Eurasia and North America, following abundant herds of prey. They shared the land with human hunters, who developed their own ideas about wolf beginnings. Some North American Native legends tell of wolves helping to create the world or bringing humans into it. Wolves also had their place in ancient skies. Both the ancient Chinese and North America's Pawnee people envisioned a wolf when they gazed at Sirius, the Dog Star. Norwegians linked the wolf and the wind. Greeks associated wolves with both wind and sun.

Whether viewed through the lens of science or the window of legend, the story of wolf beginnings makes one thing clear: humans and wolves shared a special relationship from the time they first met.

In a world older and more complete than ours they move finished and complete, gifted with extensions of the senses we have lost or never attained, living by voices we shall never hear. They are not brethren, they are not underlings; they are other nations, caught with ourselves in the net of life and time, fellow prisoners of the splendor and travail of the earth.

—Henry Beston, *The Outermost House*

The wolf of our recent past and present goes by many names including gray wolf, arctic wolf, timber wolf, tundra wolf; all these names refer to the same species, *Canis lupus.* For simplicity's sake, we'll use "gray wolf" or "wolf" to stand for all of them. The Canidae family is broken into groups of similar animals, and the wolf belongs to the group, or genus, Canis. Its closest relative may be curled up near your feet as you read this: *Canis familiaris* (the domestic dog). Other near relatives include coyotes (*Canis latrans*), red wolves (*Canis rufus*) and Ethiopian wolves (*Canis simensis*, also known as Simien jackals). Other wolflike canids include the golden jackal (*Canis aureus*), the African wild dog (*Lycaon pictus*) and the dhole (*Cuon alpinus*).

Until recently, scientists divided the North American wolf population into 24 subspecies based on skull shape, coat texture and color, and body measurements. Newer studies have resulted in several proposals for a much smaller number of subspecies, but there is disagreement on what the sorting criteria should be. Part of the problem is that some stages of the evolutionary sequence of the dog family, as well as the exact relationships between species, are not perfectly clear. Most scientists, however, agree on the early chapters of the story.

About 55 million years ago, a group of primitive carnivores called miacids appeared. These animals, which ranged from rat-sized to dog-sized, eventually gave rise to many lineages including the dog, cat and bear families. About 30 to 40 million years ago, an ancestor of the dog family called *Cynodictis* emerged. It had an elongated weasel-shaped body and was smaller than today's wolf. Over the next 15 million years, descendants of *Cynodictis* continued to evolve, becoming larger with longer legs and feet and gradually growing more wolflike in their body proportions. Scientific opinion begins to diverge concerning the next major step in the process, the emergence of the genus Canis about seven to ten million years ago.

Some scientists believe that Canis appeared first in North America, later spreading to South America and Eurasia. Others scientists say members of this genus originated in Asia and then extended their range to North America. And while scientists concur that the gray wolf came to North America from Eurasia, they have differing opinions on when this happened. Some place the event at about 750,000 years ago but a recent study suggests a different date — about 300,000 years ago.

A group of scientists headed by P. J. Wilson of Trent University collected and compared DNA samples from eastern Canadian gray wolves, gray wolves from other parts of North America, coyotes and red wolves (*Canis rufus*). Their results indicated that the eastern gray wolf and the red wolf are more closely related to each other than either is to the western gray wolf. In fact, the two may be the same species. Eastern gray wolves are also more closely related to coyotes than to western wolves. To Wilson and his group, this suggests that about one to two million years ago, a common ancestor to gray wolves, eastern North American wolves and coyotes lived in North America. They believe that some of these ancestral animals crossed the Bering land bridge into Eurasia and evolved into the gray wolf, which appeared there about one million years ago. Coyotes, eastern gray wolves and red wolves evolved from the animals that remained in North America. This theory — and much about the wolf's evolutionary past — is still being debated. Hopefully, future fossil discoveries and DNA research will help clarify the wolf's family history.

After gray wolves came back to their ancestral home in North America, they shared the continent and its prey with dire wolves (*Canis dirus*) for hundreds of thousands of years. A relative of the gray wolf, the dire wolf possessed larger teeth and jaws and was more powerfully built. At the end of the last Ice Age, about 10,000 to 20,000 years ago, climate change caused the decline and disappearance

Wisagatcak and Wolf When the World Began

Wisagatcak the Trickster was determined to catch the giant beaver. He built a dam across the creek where the beaver lived and waited for the beaver to emerge at nightfall. Just as the beaver approached, however, a muskrat bit the Trickster, causing him to miss his target and storm away in frustration.

The next day he took down his dam but the beavers, angered by his actions, decided to get revenge by taking down all of their dams as well. The waters flowed unceasingly, covering all before them until there was no earth to be seen.

Only a few survivors, including Wisagatcak, clung to a raft. After two weeks, the muskrat tried to dive to the bottom of the waters, but they were too deep and he drowned. A raven flew out to look but could spy no land.

Finally, Wisagatcak called to the wolf for help. The wolf took a ball of moss in his mouth and began to run around the raft. As he raced around and around, the ball of moss grew larger and earth began to form on it.

The wolf put the moss ball down and all the animals danced around it, singing their strongest spells. The patches of earth grew and grew. Earth soon covered the raft and spread out into the water, growing until finally it remade the whole world.

—*Cree legend*

of many species. Probably doomed by a lack of suitable prey, dire wolves faded from the scene, finally becoming extinct about 7,000 years ago. Gray wolves, on the other hand, not only survived the challenges of the new environment, but flourished: their range at one time included almost all of North America and Eurasia. Today they roam a greatly reduced portion of our world —patches of suitable habitat above latitudes 15°–20° N (roughly north of a line around the globe passing through Bombay, Mexico City and Kingston, Jamaica)— but look much the same as when our ancestors first saw them.

Human beings have always used their knowledge and imagination to create an explanation for what they see and experience. Wolves were a part of everyday life for early humans, so it's not surprising that they came up with their own ideas about the origins of wolves and of the human—wolf relationship.

The Hitchiti people of the American Southeast said that a shaman made wolves by striking together two pine cones. The creatures that appeared were weak but the shaman made them stronger by blowing on his hands then rubbing the animals. The shaman told the wolves to go where man was and to eat what he ate. Later, he regretted his action but could not take back his words. Ever after, so the legend goes, man and wolf would live in conflict.

The Inuit near Hudson Bay in Canada told of a poor mother with many children. She struggled ceaselessly to find enough food for them to eat, but they starved, and grew thinner and thinner. Finally the family was changed into wolves, constantly traveling across the land, searching for food to fill their empty stomachs. According to the legend, the howls of the mother crying in pain and distress can still be heard at night.

Wolves not only howled in the darkness at our firelight's edge but, as some stories tell, were present long before that, before us — when the edge of the world was formed.

Wolf floated alone on primeval waters while he created the earth, according to some of the Paiute people of the Great Basin. Because of this, the Kaibab Southern Paiute regarded Wolf as the most important of all beings. The Arikara people of the Great Plains told a similar story in which Wolf-Man, who made the prairies, and Lucky-Man were the creators of the earth. One version of a Northern Shoshone creation story tells how Wolf and Coyote stood together in an upper world, throwing down soil into the water covering the world. The Chemehuevi (southernmost Southern Paiute) people say that Ocean Woman stretched out the land before her and then told Wolf and Coyote to see how far it extended.

The Yokuts people of California believed that the wolf was one of the animals present at the very beginning of the world, when only water could be seen. It was the wolf's shouts that made the new earth finally stand firm. When the Pueblo people of the Southwest emerged into this world, they could not live upon the wet, soft land. Their mother creator, Ut'set, sent wolf, bear, badger and shrew to harden the earth with their magic. The Tonkawa people of the Southern Plains said that their ancestors were freed from the imprisoning earth by Wolf scratching away at the dirt. They commemorated this event with a dance in which dancers in wolfskins scratched at the ground and finally unearthed a previously concealed Tonkawa man.

The Lakota people of the Northern Plains say it was a wolf who led the first of their people from under the earth through a cave into this world. Wolf was also present when the Caddo people, who lived in the American Southeast, emerged. In their story, he sealed up the entrance to this

Although the Norse god, Odin, had two wolf companions—Geri (Hungry) and Freki (Ravenous)—he was fated to be devoured by another wolf, Fenrir, when the world came to an end. Wolves play a prominent role in Norse mythology, usually symbolizing death and destruction.

world before all of the people and animals had come out, trapping some of them underground.

Ancient wolves were earth makers and earth movers, but not earthbound. An old Norwegian riddle asks, "Who is the wolf who sits on the blue vault of heaven and howls out to sea?" The answer: the wind. Observing a field of grain rippling with wind-bred waves, the people of many European countries spoke of a wolf traveling through the rye. An Inuit story tells of a wolf calling up a freezing wind by howling. This association is easily explained: huddled up on a winter night with a blizzard howling outside, one might envision a giant ravenous wolf racing over the snow-swept land.

The ancient Greeks called the vapors that issue from the ground in volcanic regions "wolf" and believed these had special powers. Temples were often built at these fumaroles, and oracles who inhaled the fumes prophesied the future. Interestingly enough, recent analysis of water taken from springs near one of these sites showed traces of ethylene, a gas that can induce a floating sensation and euphoria, and that once was used as an anesthetic.

The Greek god Apollo was sometimes called Apollo Lykeios, the wolf-Apollo. He was associated with the wind and the sun. Greek myths related that a wolf came to the goddess Leto while she was pregnant with Apollo, transferring its spirit to her unborn child. In Athens, the land surrounding the temple of Apollo became known as the Lyceum, the "wolfskin."

Some of the oldest Scandinavian myths tell of two wolves: Sköll, who chases the sun and tries to devour it, and Hati, who does the same with the moon. Eclipses were said to happen when the wolves came close to success. At those times, people would bang on pots and pans, making as much noise as possible, to frighten the wolf away.

The Crow people living near the Yellowstone River and its tributaries, in Montana and Wyoming, told of

White Wolf, a servant of Sun. He helped the people to find food when Sun was angry with them and banished them from their land. Seeing that they were starving, White Wolf taught them a ceremony that produced ten fat buffalo. He warned them that all the buffalo must be killed because any that escaped would run to Sun and tell what Wolf had done. At first everything went well, but eventually a single buffalo escaped and went immediately to Sun. Sun became very angry, not at the people, who had been brave despite their hunger, but at Wolf, who had worked against his master. Sun told the Crow people that he would no longer punish them. Wolf, however, declared Sun, was forever more to be a wanderer, an outcast among all the world's animals.

High in the heavens, the "Dog Star" Sirius held lupine meaning for two widely separated groups of people. In China, it was called the Celestial Wolf, and was believed to guard a great palace in the constellation of Ursa Major. The Pawnee people of the Great Plains, known to neighboring tribes as the Wolf People, called this star Fools-the-Wolf because at times it rises just before the morning star, deceiving wolves into howling before dawn. They also called it simply the Wolf Star and told how it was responsible for humans living, not in the sky as eternal stars, but on Earth as mortals.

Both the Blackfoot and Pawnee referred to the Milky Way as the Wolf Road, and believed it led to the spirit world. The Pawnee explained the seasonal appearance and disappearance of Sirius, the Wolf Star, as the wolf travelling the starry road between this world and the next.

The ancient Chinese believed that a wolf guarded the celestial palace found in the constellation of Ursa Major.

Gray wolf effigy pipe from Tremper Mound, Ohio. Created by the Hopewell people sometime between 100–200 AD.

According to the words of the Chao hun (a third-century B.C. poem by Sung Yu), "a wolf with piercing eyes comes and goes and slowly throws men into the air and plays ball with them. He tosses them into a deep abyss, in obedience to his Lord, and then he may go to sleep."

Skiri, also written as Skidi, was a name sometimes applied to all of the Pawnee. However, it referred particularly to the people of the Skiri band, who lived in the village of Skirirara. They were the keepers of the Wolf Bundle, which was wrapped in a wolfskin and topped with a wolf skull. The Skiri said they learned their ceremonies from the star that gave them the bundle and its contents. One of their ceremonies involved sacrificing a human to the Morning Star. A man representing the Wolf Star played a major role in the raid to capture a victim, and then cared for the person who was to be sacrificed until the Morning Star priest decided that the night skies indicated the time was right.

Viewing the wolves that shared their world with respect and admiration, early people created myths and legends about primeval wolves and their powers. Some people, like the Skiri, credited the wolf with a major role in bringing humans to Earth. Others believed a wolf created the earth itself. Science confirms that wolves lived in the distant past, tracing their lineage back millions of years. They had already been here a long time when humans appeared. From our earliest association with them, wolves have played a unique part in our lives and imaginations. Scientists and storytellers agree: humans and wolves had — and still have — an intimate and evolving relationship.

Haida wolf mask used for dancing. The wolf's teeth are abalone shell and the irises of its eyes are inlaid haliotis shell. In each ear is a carved bear figure.

How the Skiri People Came to Be

In the earliest days of the world, Tirawa the Great Creator sent Lightning to explore the land. On his back Lightning carried a sack made from a tornado, which held stars he had chosen from the many in the sky. After a long day spent exploring, Lightning sat down to rest. He was lonely, so he opened his sack and released the stars to keep him company. Out they tumbled, each running on two legs. They set up camps that sparkled on the darkened land.

Each morning, Lightning gathered the stars back into his whirlwind sack and each evening he released them. The star people might have lived always this way and been an immortal race, but, high above, the Wolf Star watched with growing anger. Earlier the gods had forgotten to invite him to a great council meeting about how creation should happen. Now they had placed creatures on the earth without asking his opinion. Very well, he would send a creature of his own.

The Wolf Star made a wolf and set it upon the land, telling it to find Lightning and steal his star-filled sack. When the wolf eventually caught up with him, Lightning had fallen asleep after a long day. The sack lay unopened beside him. Quickly and quietly, the wolf snatched the bag and began to run off with it. But as it bumped along the ground, the bag flew open and star people came spilling out. Angry at the rough ride and frightened to see a creature they did not understand, the star people killed the wolf.

The noise they made woke Lightning, who shook his head in dismay. "You have killed this being without my permission. If you had not done this, I might have carried you on my back forever. Instead, you have brought death into this world and you will live here with it from now on. You must take the skin of this wolf, tan it and use it to wrap a sacred bundle in which you will keep things to remind you of this day. More creatures like this one you have killed will appear. They will be known as Skirihk (Thief) and you will be called Skiri (Carry-Wolf's-Hide)."

—*Pawnee myth*

At lower left is the star Sirius (Alpha Canis Majoris). This is the brightest star in the sky (excluding the Sun), and is also known as the Dog Star.

Now this is the law of the jungle,
as old and as true as the sky,

And the wolf that shall keep it may prosper,
but the wolf that shall break it must die.

As the creeper that girdles the tree trunk,
the law runneth forward and back;

For the strength of the pack is the wolf,
and the strength of the wolf is the pack.

— *Rudyard Kipling*

PART OF THE PACK

Highly adaptable individuals who rely on group effort to survive — that phrase applies equally well to both humans and wolves. Much of wolves' ecological flexibility — gray wolves at one time made their homes in all major habitats including desert, swamp, forest, prairie and tundra — stems from the cooperative nature of the pack. This quality is evident with the birth of each new pack member. All wolves in the pack work to feed and care for the initially helpless young. As the cubs grow, they explore their world under the watchful eyes of the pack and learn the communication skills required by its social structure. When greeting one another, wolves use a variety of postures to indicate dominance or submission. They leave scent marks at territory boundaries and use their howls for long-distance communication. Cubs must master all these things and perfect their hunting skills as well. Most will leave their birth pack to find territories of their own, often joining up with other young wanderers to form new packs.

Scientists have observed the care wolf packs take with their cubs, but history contains several supposedly factual stories of wolf packs looking after not only their own young but human infants as well. The famous story of Kamala and Amala, two feral children found near Calcutta, India, has come under question but, whether it was true or not, people believed enough in the possibility to record it as fact.

Early people identified with much they saw in wolves, and their stories sought to explain the closeness they felt. Like the Dzawada'enuxw,

OPPOSITE Pack members develop strong bonds from the beginning. Wolf biologist John Theberge ranks wolf social bonding and care-giving second only to that of humans and other social primates.

Patrick Amos, *Wolf Dancer*, silkscreen.

OPPOSITE Although most wolves that leave a pack are dispersing juveniles, subordinate adults suffering continual harassment, going hungry because of food shortages, or needing to mate may also leave. These are the animals that most often become lone wolves, sometimes haunting the edge of a pack but never really part of it. Without the assistance and protection of a pack, lone wolves suffer a high mortality rate.

people of many cultures spoke of wolves as their ancestors. According to the Turks, wolves not only begat a bloodline but sired a nation. Romans told of wolves helping people in trouble and adopting human infants. In an echo of the wolves' own hierarchical pack structure, several Northwest Coast peoples used a symbolic "joining of the pack" ritual when acknowledging their young people as full-fledged members of the community.

A wolf pack usually consists of a breeding pair and their offspring from the previous one to three years. Sometimes two or three families join together. In North America, packs most often contain between four and seven animals, although scientists have documented a pack with over 30 wolves in Alaska. In Europe, packs are smaller and there seem to be more lone wolves.

Pack size is related to the abundance and size of prey. Larger packs can take down bigger prey but also require more food. They are most likely to be found where there is an abundance of large ungulates, such as elk and moose. The smaller size of European packs may be related to the smallness of most available prey, typically hares and rodents.

Each pack has a clear dominance hierarchy led by the highest-ranking male and female. Either of these may serve as pack leader, or alpha wolf, and female alphas are as common as males. Besides its place in the overall pack hierarchy, a wolf belonging to a large pack will also have a ranking among members of its own sex. Pups start at the bottom of the heap and are frequently reminded to respect their elders. The older the pack, the more stable its social structure. Position in the pack is mutable, however, and shifts as wolves mature, weaken due to illness or injury, or form alliances with other members of the pack. The hierarchy may also alter as the result of successful challenges and

confrontations by less dominant wolves. These contests for rank reach their peak during the winter breeding season.

On average, wolves become sexually mature when they are just under two years old. They mate between January and April, with those living in the north mating later than those in the south. Courtship between pack members, or between lone wolves who have found one another, happens throughout the breeding season, but the female wolf is receptive and capable of conceiving for only five to seven days. Like other members of the dog family, mating wolves become locked in a "copulatory tie" in which the swollen base of the male's penis is held tight by the female's vaginal sphincter. Surrounded by an eddy of excited pack members, the two animals may remain bound together for up to 30 minutes.

Sometimes only the top-ranking pair breeds, even though there may be other females of breeding age. The alpha female may terrorize subordinate females to keep them from breeding, sometimes by actively attacking them if they try to mate, although psychological bullying is often deterrent enough. The number of litters a pack produces depends on such factors as the availability of food and the pack mortality rate. In an area with a low wolf population and lots of prey, more pups may be born than in an area with less favorable conditions. However, in an extremely demanding habitat, such as the Arctic tundra, more females breed. Producing more offspring helps to offset high mortality rates resulting from the harsh living conditions. The same strategy is evident in packs that are hunted. If humans kill pack members, the pack attempts to compensate for the losses by allowing more of its females to breed: 90 percent of the adult females versus 60 percent in an unmolested pack.

About four to six weeks after mating, the female wolf searches for a den site within the pack's home range — the area where they live, hunt and raise their young. In

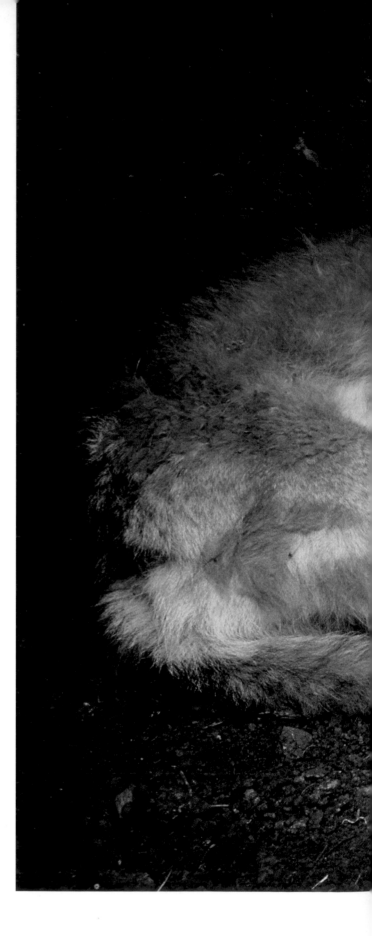

Rethinking Wolf

Our traditional picture of the wolf presents an odious creature, a monster of cruelty and destruction; actuated by nothing higher than a gluttonous appetite for food. I have learned of wolves whose master trait was wisdom. I have met many a wolf whose overwhelming motive was the love of its little ones.

—*Ernest Thompson Seton*

some cases, she may select and prepare more than one site. The most attractive properties have good drainage and a nearby water source.

The female may dig a completely new den or enlarge an existing hole made by another animal, such as a fox. Some wolves make their dens in abandoned beaver lodges, at the base of large trees, in hollow logs or in caves. Others give birth in relatively shallow surface excavations. In areas where they are left undisturbed, wolf packs may use the same den sites for many years.

The average den has a simple configuration. A mound of freshly dug dirt lies like a "welcome mat" outside an oval opening measuring about 14 to 26 inches across. Inside, a tunnel approximately the same diameter or slightly larger

extends back six to 14 feet. At the end lies a bare, enlarged chamber where newborn pups are kept. There may be additional entrances or passages, depending on the site and the preferences of the wolf.

Just over two months after mating, the female wolf retreats to the seclusion of the den. Protected from enemies and the elements, she gives birth to the newest members of the pack. About the size and weight of a pound of butter, the wet, helpless cubs can neither hear nor see. With their flat ears, pug noses and chunky little bodies, they look more like bears than wolves. Their mother licks each one as it arrives, removing the amniotic sac and birth fluids. She bites through its umbilical cord and gently nudges the newborn to her side so it can begin nurs-

Dakota Wolf Dream Song

Father, somewhere, heads home howling!
Mother, somewhere, heads home howling!
Father brings a young calf home and
Mother, somewhere, heads home howling!
Now she returns in a sacred manner, comes
    home!

This song was used for hunting. The wolf cubs are singing of a successful hunt.

ing. Unable to regulate their body temperature for some time after birth, the cubs snuggle into their mother's fur, soaking up her warmth. Because her cubs are so dependent, even requiring her help to urinate and defecate, the female stays with them in the den for the next month, seldom going out for long. During her confinement, the pack members provide room service, leaving food for her at the den entrance.

Three weeks after the cubs are born, their eyes begin to open and they sense the light at the den entrance. With many false starts and sudden naps, they lurch on wobbly legs toward the opening. Eventually, a small head emerges, blue eyes blinking at the daylight, and a cub takes its first tentative steps into the world of the pack.

The pack members take a great interest in the cubs. All play with new arrivals and help to feed them, regurgitating semisolid food for them to eat. It isn't long before the cubs greet each arriving adult excitedly, sniffing and licking at its muzzle and mouth. The adult responds by disgorging food, which the cubs gobble up. If prey is difficult to find, the adult wolf may have traveled many miles to bring home this meal.

Full of energy, the cubs romp around the den site, which begins to look pretty ragged thanks to all the activity. Feathers, bones and other dinner debris make excellent trophies to pounce on, carry proudly and growl over. Wrestling, punctuated by bursts of running, is also popular. Naps, frequent at first, are often abruptly ended by a sibling seeking a playmate. During these games, the cubs establish and reinforce their status within the pack. Already, the strongest and boldest gets the largest share of food and will have the best chance to make it through the coming winter. When the pack members play with the cubs, they show a surprising amount of patience with their antics. But if a youngster becomes too impertinent, a rough roll in the dirt quickly reminds it of its place.

TOP Wolves of all ages love to play but it is especially important for pups. As they romp with one another and with adults, wolf pups develop strength and hunting skills, sort out their place in the pack and learn to communicate with pack members.

BOTTOM Carried around proudly or defended with a small growl, a wolf pup's trophy may be a feather, bone, plant or just about anything else the pup fancies.

By six to nine weeks of age, the cubs are no longer nursing. Now the pack moves away from the tattered den site and begins to use a series of rendezvous sites. These sites serve as a "daycare" area where the cubs are left, usually in the care of an adult, while the rest of the pack looks for food. Juvenile pack members sometimes stay behind and may share whatever small prey they capture with the cubs. In turn, the juveniles usually manage to get some of the food the adults bring back. If the wolves make a large kill that can feed the pack for several meals, such as a moose, the pack may all move to the kill site rather than dragging the meat back piece by piece. They may continue to use the new location as a rendezvous point even after the carcass is picked clean.

The cubs progress from partly digested food to small whole animals. At first, they receive only dead prey but eventually they are given half-alive prey on which they can practice their hunting skills. By the time they are seven or eight months old, the cubs will be hunting for small prey on their own. At this stage, the once-tiny cubs have nearly reached their full adult size and weight. An adult male wolf may weigh from 45 to 175 pounds and measure four to six feet from nose to tail tip. Adult females are smaller.

This extended childhood, longer than that of many animals, is necessary for the cubs to develop their survival skills. It also provides the time for strong bonds to form between the cubs and the rest of the pack. Hunting as a group, sharing food, constantly touching and playing with one another — these everyday activities strengthen the social structure that holds the pack together. All of this interaction requires communication, and wolves have evolved a complex language of posture, gesture, sound and scent.

In close situations, wolves rely on each other's postures, facial expressions and gestures to tell them what's happening. If you have ever watched a dog bow when it

wants to play or wrinkle its brow in puzzlement over a strange sound, you can understand how clear wordless communication can be. How a wolf holds its head and ears, carries its tail and positions its body all send a message. Watching the interactions of a pack when they meet one another is fascinating. A submissive wolf greeting a dominant one will thrust its muzzle toward that of the other, much like a cub begging for food. The expression "running away with your tail tucked between your legs" perfectly describes the reaction of a wolf responding to a challenge by a higher-ranking animal. All of this activity may be accompanied by whining, growling and barking.

For long-distance communication, wolves rely on scent and sound. Wolves have an extremely acute sense of smell. It is probably their strongest sense. Wolf biologist L. David Mech reported that wolves he was observing usually scented moose from about 300 yards away, but that he once observed them sniff out a cow moose and her twin calves from over a mile and a half downwind.

Taking advantage of this ability, wolves leave aromatic advertisements wherever they go.

Odors left behind by scent glands in their paws mark a trail as they travel. Other wolves crossing this path up to three days later will notice it. Urine marks, which convey readiness to breed as well as declaring "this turf is occupied," are left on landmarks like tree stumps and rocks. Ernest Thompson Seton, in *Great Historic Animals*, wrote, "The behaviour of a wolf arriving at one of these smell-posts is precisely like that of a man coming to his club after an absence. He goes to the register, glances at the page, adds his own record, then makes a more elaborate study of those who came before, recognizes friends and acquaintances, and notes the time of arrival . . ." Although a club member would certainly be frowned upon if he "added his own record" in the same manner as a wolf, the description is a good one.

Scent-marking with urine is a form of wolf communication. Often, only the alpha male urinates with a raised leg. Females and subordinate males squat. Scent marks serve as "no trespassing" signs at territory boundaries and wolf packs mark more frequently when they come across signs of other packs.

OPPOSITE Wolves show strong, long-lasting mate preferences, usually giving the brush-off to suitors other than their chosen partner. Should something happen to that partner, however, a wolf may shift its attentions to another.

Tlingit crest hat.

There is nothing on earth like a lone wolf call — it makes you draw a little closer to the fire, dig a little deeper into your blanket and shudder, knowing in your heart the many things you'll never know.

— *Trapper Herbert Andrus*

OPPOSITE Somehow, even across great distance, lone wolves manage to sniff each other out. In 1982 the only male wolf in Scandinavia tracked down the lone female of his kind.

For longer-lasting marks, wolves leave behind feces. Smelly enough on its own, wolf scat gets added punch from the particularly pungent secretions of glands located just inside the anus. This pheromone-packed substance is a scent "fingerprint" that identifies the individual depositor. Territory edges, which often overlap those of neighboring packs by about half a mile, are heavily marked; a wolf in the overlap area can sniff out clear boundary lines. Using urine and feces in this way reduces the number of dangerous face-to-face encounters needed to defend a pack's territory.

To humans, wolf howls are mysterious, eerie and romantic. For wolves, howling is another activity that binds the pack together. Sometimes they appear to howl purely for the joy of it, while at other times anxiety may be the spur, as when lost pups howl until a pack member comes to find them. Howls from outside the pack, whether from a neighboring pack or a group of human imitators, receive a howl in reply less than 50 percent of the time — perhaps because it is not always a good idea to let everyone know exactly where you are. Wolves howl less during early summer, when they are all meeting frequently at the den. In winter, as breeding season nears and tensions in the pack rise, howling becomes much more frequent. Lone wolves, too, cast their voices on the icy winds, hoping to find a mate.

Young wolves usually spend their first winter, when their hunting skills are minimal, with the pack. However, they are more likely to be transient pack members than the breeding adults. Most young wolves begin to disperse, or leave their pack's territory, when they are one to two years old, although records show wolves as young as nine months departing. They may travel great distances at this time — one yearling female covered over 500 miles — but most end up joining or forming packs 30 to 60 miles from where they were born. Most new packs are probably created by these young animals joining forces.

from **Wolves and Wilderness**

For some, wolf music is as deeply moving as
Beethoven's Fifth Symphony reverberating
in the chambers of a great concert hall.
For others, it is a call to arms, stirring up
mad hate, blind terror. It both symbolizes
the modern movement to preserve some
wilderness and mocks man that he hasn't
conquered it all.

—*John B. Theberge*

Wolves at Our Doors: The Domestic Dog

It is difficult to look at Fifi the poodle and imagine a wolf at the base of her family tree. But he is there, nonetheless. Exactly when and where humans adopted the wolf into their pack is unknown. About 12,000 years ago in what is now Israel, a group of hunter-gatherers buried a body with its hand resting on a pup. But whether the bones are those of a wolf or a dog is impossible to tell. Until recently, most scientists placed the domestication of the dog somewhere in the Middle East between 10,000 and 15,000 years ago. Archaeological evidence tends to support this approximate date. However, a 1997 study of mitochondrial DNA sequences from 140 dogs and 162 wolves confirmed that wolves were indeed the ancestors of dogs but put the split much farther back—more than 100,000 years ago. Many scientists questioned assumptions used in the study while others found it convincing.

A similar study used a larger data set — samples from 654 dogs from around the world. The results suggested that dogs originated about 15,000 years ago from several different female wolf lineages but possibly from a single wolf population. The place of origin was almost certainly East Asia.

Yet another DNA study showed that the first people who came to the Americas via the Bering land bridge about 12,000 to 14,000 years ago brought their dogs along.

Although scientists continue to discuss the evidence and look for new ways to investigate, one thing is clear: humans have valued canine companionship for a long time.

Forged in cubhood, the bonds between members of a wolf pack are strong. Do those bonds ever extend to an outsider, a member of a different species, a human? The historical record contains several accounts of wolf-raised feral children, beginning with the German Wolf Child of Hesse in 1344. India has an unusual abundance of these stories.

The most heavily publicized account of Indian wolf-children began in 1920, when searchers discovered two young girls, Kamala and Amala, living in a wolf den near Calcutta. Reports from the orphanage where they were taken said that the girls could not talk, ate only raw meat, lapped up liquids and disliked daylight. Later authors questioned the reliability of information about the girls and their origins, and a look at the evidence in light of modern knowledge reveals that those "wolflike" behaviors are often seen in autistic or abused children. At the time, however, the girls were considered marvelous examples of a long-held belief that wolves were capable of raising human children.

In 1972, a cyclist in a forest near Sultanpur noticed movement in the underbrush. To his surprise, he saw it was caused by several wolf cubs playing alongside a child. The man captured the four-year-old boy after a struggle, tied him to the bicycle and took him to the nearby village of Narayanpur. The boy lived there, cared for by his captor's family, until 1978. He was then taken to Lucknow, where he stayed at a home run by Mother Theresa until he died eight years later.

Could these stories be true? Dogs have adopted kittens, piglets and even tiger cubs. They have kept lost or abandoned children safe and warm until rescuers arrived. Canadian wolf researcher Paul Paquet reported that a female wolf in Banff National Park, Alberta, successfully adopted and raised four orphaned wolf pups. Although she was never pregnant, the wolf was able to lactate and nursed the pups. If a wolf was unable to lactate, she might still regurgitate partially digested food to feed a baby just as she does for her pups. Theoretically, then, a wolf might be drawn to and be able to care for a human infant, at least temporarily. Until concrete proof of such an event appears, the scientific community remains unconvinced.

Early people, on the other hand, had no problem imagining an intimate relationship between wolves and humans. Those who visualized a wolf at the beginning of their bloodline might have traced the relationship back to a direct transformation as the Kwakiutl did, or to a coupling between wolf and human. A Bella Coola (Nuxalk) tale tells the story of a man who marries a wolf in human form. He ill-treats her by paying attention to another woman but eventually convinces her of his love. They stay together with their child in the wolf village and the man becomes a real wolf. In Kamchatka, people assumed the wolf was the father of one of any twins that were born. They made a wolf figure each fall to encourage the wolf to keep fertilizing the women of the village for another year.

The belief that wolves married and mated with humans is difficult for modern human beings to understand. The people who told these stories, however, saw the world differently. To them, there was little or no difference between animals and humans. Both struggled to survive in a world filled with inexplicable events and with physical and spiritual dangers. Drawing on the special skills and powers possessed by another creature was a way to improve the odds of survival. Visualizing the highly

Kwakiutl Wolf/Raven Transformation Mask. The outer face is a wolf. The wearer pulls the strings to open the face into two equal parts, revealing a raven's face with a beak that opens and closes.

The Origin of the Chipewyan and Inuit People

A young mother with two children was trying desperately to escape from her enemies. After traveling fast for many hours, they reached the shore of a great lake and the mother sank to her knees in despair. Without a canoe, she and her children were trapped.

A wolf appeared on the shore, wagging his tail. Several times he walked out into the water and then came back to her, as if trying to tell her to follow him. Finally, the wolf came to her and licked the tears from her face. He looked at the water, took a few steps and looked back at the woman.

Surely they would all drown, she thought, but if they stayed here they would be killed. On trembling legs, the woman led her children into the lake. As they continued to walk farther out, the woman was amazed to find that the water never rose above her ankles. After two days of walking they finally reached the far shore. Although they were exhausted, they were safe now, thanks to the wolf.

And what a difference their rescue would make to the world, for the oldest boy was destined to become the father of the Eskimo (Inuit) people, while from his younger brother would come the Chipewyan people.

—*Déné myth*

adaptable, predatory wolf as an ancestor who passed on many admirable traits made sense, especially if you lived in a society in which hunters or warriors enjoyed high status. Genghis Khan, Mongol conqueror and founder of an empire that eventually spanned the continent of Asia, traced his family tree back to a mating between a white doe and a gray wolf.

The Founding of the Turkish Nation
TURKISH LEGEND

Long ago, the ancestors of the Turks lived at the edge of a large swamp. Enemies descended upon them, killing all but a ten-year-old boy. A she-wolf found the wounded youth and carried him off into the mountains. When he was grown, he took the wolf as his wife. Each of the ten sons she bore him married a local woman. The greatest of the sons became the founder of a new tribe which, along with the other descendants of the she-wolf, moved into the Altai of northwestern Mongolia and took the name Turk.

The Turks not only claimed the wolf as an ancestor but also cast it in two other even more intriguing roles: rescuer and adoptive parent. They were not alone. Many cultures, including the Déné (Chipewyan) people of subarctic Canada, portray the wolf as a savior of those in trouble.

The Dakota (Sioux) of the Great Plains tell of a wolf who saved a disobedient hunter from the ghosts sent to kill him in the night. Another Dakota story tells how a young wife fled a cruel husband. She met a wolf in the form of a man who took her to his village. There she lived for a year, fed and cared for by the wolves, before returning to her own people.

One of the most well-known stories of wolves saving a human in need originated in the mind of a Victorian author. Rudyard Kipling took his Victorian beliefs about fair play and clean living, wrote them into ripping good yarns about animals and published them in 1894 and 1895 as *The Jungle Books.* In 1916, one of the tales, "Mowgli's Brothers"—the story of a boy adopted by a wolf pack, inspired Robert Baden-Powell to form an organization called the Wolf Cubs for young British boys. Why choose a wild wolf-child as a role model? Appealing to a boy's sense of adventure, the stories stirred an interest in nature and outdoor activities. Baden-Powell also felt that Kipling's portrayal of the wolf's world, showing the submission of each individual to a set of rules and hierarchies, set a good example for children. Baden-Powell used names from the story for positions in each chapter, or pack, of his group, now known as the Cub Scouts. For example, the Cubmaster is known as Akela (the Father Wolf and pack leader) while an Assistant Cubmaster may be called Baloo (the Bear) or Bagheera (the Panther). Even today, part of Mowgli's story is included in the Cub Scout book.

Tales of wolves adopting and caring for human infants were common in Europe and Asia, where infanticide by exposure was sometimes a method of dealing with unwanted children. In legends, the rescued child grew up to be especially strong or brave. Siegfried, the great Teutonic hero, and Miletus, son of the god Apollo and founder of the ancient western Turkish city that bore his name, were two babes suckled by wolf nurses. Perhaps the most famous example is the story of Romulus and Remus, who grew up to found the city of Rome.

The idea of a wolf as foster parent seemed remarkable even to those who recorded it as factual history. Ovid, a Roman poet who lived from about 43 B.C. to A.D. 17, wrote about the story of Romulus and Remus: "A she-wolf which had cast her whelps came, wondrous to tell, to the abandoned twins: who could believe that the brute would not harm the boys? Far from harming, she helped them;

The Story of Romulus and Remus

Rhea Silvia, a Vestal Virgin and daughter of a king, became pregnant by the god Mars, who appeared one night in her chambers in the form of a giant phallus. Her uncle, Amulius, had forced his brother from the throne and was enraged by the possibility of offspring that would continue the true royal lineage. As soon as Rhea gave birth to twin sons, Amulius ordered that they be left by the River Tiber to die from exposure. The boys, Romulus and Remus, were saved from death by a she-wolf who suckled them and cared for them until a shepherd named Faustulus found them.

Faustulus and his wife raised the boys, who grew to be strong, noble and courageous young men. Eventually, their real identity was revealed. Romulus and Remus deposed Amulius and restored their grandfather to his rightful place. Then they left to build a city of their own. An argument arose between the twins over some details of the city's construction and in a fiery rage Romulus murdered his brother. In 753 B.C., the new city, Rome, was founded on ground soaked with the blood of brother slain by brother — an inauspicious beginning for one of the world's great cities.

—Greek legend

Group of dancers in ceremonial costume for what is described as the "wolf dance of the Kaviagamutes" of coastal Alaska. Little appears to have been recorded about this particular ceremony but the importance of the wolf is clear. Photo c. 1903–1915.

and they whom ruthless kinsfolk would have killed with their own hands were suckled by a wolf!"

The she-wolf came to the boys' assistance when all who should have cared for them had turned away. She accepted them into the pack. Why did so many people tell this tale and why were others so eager to believe it? Perhaps because it was comforting to believe there was a creature that would care for those whom civilized human society had unjustly rejected.

Joining a pack, becoming one of a social group, has always been an important part of human experience. Observing the close-knit, altruistic nature of the wolf pack may have led some cultures to invoke the wolf's presence during rituals that marked the passage from child to community member. The Nootka (Nuu-chah-nulth), Kwakiutl (Kwakwaka'wakw), Makah and Quillayute of the Pacific Northwest each performed an elaborate wolf initiation ritual, usually at the beginning of winter. Each had unique characteristics, described in great detail by Alice Henson Ernst in *The Wolf Ritual of the Northwest Coast*; however, the Nootka initiation ceremony contained the core elements common to all.

Called the Tluukwaana, the ceremony centered around an ancient legend of a young hero, Yanamhum, stolen from his people by wolves. After trying but failing to kill Yanamhum, the wolves taught him the secrets of their society. Then they sent him back to his people with instructions to pass on his new knowledge.

At the beginning of the Tluukwaana, the Wolves (members of the Wolf Society) gathered and prepared for their task. In ancient times they spread wolfskins across their backs; later they substituted dark blankets for the pelts. The Wolves captured people to be initiated, usually boys and girls about seven or eight years old, and took them to a secluded Wolf House. After receiving several days of training about their heritage, values and responsibilities as members of the Wolf Society, the initiates were returned to the village. They acted wild, as though possessed by spirits. To drive away the spirits and recover the initiates, the people held a series of ceremonies designed to "calm the Wolf." Dancers, their roles determined by hereditary right, used different masks and postures to portray the changing moods of the wolf as he was calmed.

First came the Crawling Wolves, who crawled on hands and knees once around the fire. Later came the Whirling or Spinning Wolves, who danced in a rapid whirling movement, always from left to right. Last was the Standing Wolf, representing the wolf in his most benevolent incarnation. A celebration of the initiates' rescue from the Wolves followed.

Having demonstrated the new dances and songs they had learned, the initiates were ready to take up their role as community and society members. As Nelson Keitlah from Ahousaht declared, "The Tluukwaana is awesome and sacred. It is what governs our society. Going through it changes your life."

All wolf initiation rituals of the Pacific Northwest peoples involved reenactment of a similar legend, possession and reclamation of the initiates, and the gaining of powers or instructions from the wolves. The Kwakiutl name for the ceremony, Klukwalle, meant "to find a treasure," referring to obtaining gifts from a spirit.

Why was the wolf chosen to play such an important role? Symbolizing bravery and endurance, the wolf served as a potential source of these qualities for people whose survival often depended on possessing them. Wolf ceremonies grew from an ancient human longing for supernatural help in a world filled with uncertainty and mystery.

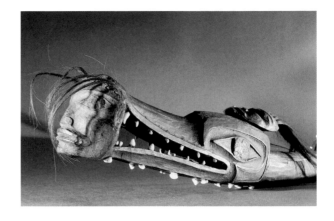

Nootka (Nuu-chah-nulth) Ceremonial Club. Used during the Wolf Dance, the club depicts a wolf carrying off an uninitiated person.

Nisga'a Wolf Rattle. A small wolf head is carved between the ears. The body of the wolf — back legs and tail — are carved on the back face of the rattle.

The wolf pack copes with uncertainty by drawing upon its cooperative strength. Together, pack members care for the young, tending to their needs, and teaching them essential hunting and communication skills. Early people believed that this caring nature could reach out to include humans in need. They felt a kinship with the wolf and explained it in stories of wolf ancestors and caregivers. Some groups used the wolf's loyalty to the pack as a model for young people joining the adult community. Ancient kinship stories and facts revealed by research tell the same tale: for both early humans and wolves, life was more secure when you were part of the pack.

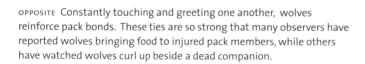

OPPOSITE Constantly touching and greeting one another, wolves reinforce pack bonds. These ties are so strong that many observers have reported wolves bringing food to injured pack members, while others have watched wolves curl up beside a dead companion.

Wolves Taught the Tsistsistas to Hunt

When the Tsistsistas (Cheyenne) people first moved onto the tall grasslands of the prairies they did not know the proper way to hunt and could find no game. They were starving.

Taking pity upon them, the spirits sent a white wolf and a red wolf to the people. Master hunters of the grasslands, the wolves taught the Tsistsistas proper hunting ways.

Ever after in thanks, the people called wolves to their kills, just as the wolves call the ravens, and left meat for them.

—*Tsistsistas legend*

LEGENDARY PREDATOR

For most people, the wolf equals predator, and indeed wolves are superb hunters. Over thousands of years, wolves have acted as a selective pressure on the prey they pursue, part of the intricately patterned dance of evolution. During the Ice Age, wolves were one of the two dominant predators following the vast grazing herds. Their way of life, from hunting habits to social structure, was mirrored by that of the second predator — humans.

Nomadic hunters themselves, early people respected wolves and envied their skills. Many cultures spoke of wolves teaching people to hunt, sometimes by direct instruction and sometimes by humans imitating what they saw wolves doing. Although humans eventually developed weapons that enabled them to choose among the prime animals of the herd, wolves still select the most vulnerable prey — the young, old or weak. They take large ungulates when they can find them but feed on a wide variety of other creatures. Scientists are still investigating how wolves affect the numbers of their prey — a pertinent query for human hunters and wildlife managers. Besides their direct impact on prey populations, wolves exert a variety of influences on their environment, including secondary effects, like increased shrub growth along streams, that one might never imagine.

Wolves' predatory nature inevitably brought them into conflict with humans, who had given up the nomadic hunting lifestyle for an agrarian

Blackfoot hunters sang to invite wolves along on their hunts, believing the animals' presence would bring them luck.

one that included domesticating useful animals. Humans took the wolf, magnified it through a lens of fear, and created a slavering, ravenous beast. Occasional attacks by rabid wolves probably helped to build this myth, but documented cases of healthy wolves attacking humans are quite rare.

From admired predator to feared killer is quite a journey for an animal whose behavior changed very little, if at all. The transformation begins during the most recent major glaciation — commonly called the Ice Ages — which occurred 1.6 million to 10,000 years ago.

🐾

When we talk about the Ice Ages, our minds create a picture of omnipresent glaciers and windswept, snow-covered landscapes. In reality, periods of glaciation alternated with interglacial periods, during which temperatures in many places rose higher than they are now. Even during glacial periods, summer brought warm temperatures that allowed the growth of vegetation much like that found in Central Europe today.

As local temperatures rose and fell, plants and animals did not simply wink in and out of existence when the heat or cold exceeded their tolerance. Instead, they migrated to new zones of viability. Animals like the reindeer made seasonal migrations over an area that shifted north or south depending on whether the prevailing climate was glacial or interglacial. Plants, of course, did not have the same ease of mobility but, because the climate changes were gradual, their ranges also shifted in latitude and altitude. Present-day scientists are beginning to see southern plants extending their ranges northward as our planet experiences global warming.

The stage was set for the coming of the grazing herds. Forest cover disappeared in many places, replaced by open

Raven follows wolf. Wolf follows caribou. Inuit hunters searching for a caribou herd relied on their knowledge of animal behavior, using ravens and wolves as pathfinders.

plains. Well watered by melting ice in summer, these vast expanses became vast repositories of food. Animals that had been browsing among the trees of the forest evolved to take advantage of this new opportunity. The predators that trailed them were forced to develop new strategies and evolve new physical characteristics to cope with conditions in the exposed terrain.

One group of hunters came from canid bloodstock. They grew bigger and faster, and developed a social organization that allowed and rewarded cooperation. The modern wolf, as it appeared in North America about a million years ago, was a physically formidable predator. It was swift and possessed an exceptionally keen sense of smell. Its powerful teeth and jaws were designed for gripping and tearing flesh, and for crushing bones.

The other main predator following the herds seemed negligible in comparison. Descended from tree-dwelling primates, this hunter had a comparatively poor sense of smell but keen sight. Running on two legs, this primate was slow and lacked stamina, but its other two limbs ended in hands capable of making and manipulating tools. It could make weapons, which compensated for its weak jaws and teeth. It lacked the warm fur of the wolf but covered itself with the skins of the animals it hunted and warmed itself by fires. This human hunter could reason and plan ahead. It shared with the wolf an intelligence and social organization that used cooperative effort to achieve goals unattainable for an individual.

Early humans and wolves both lived in small family groups and raised offspring that needed a long learning period before becoming contributing members of the community. All group members shared the available food, including the young and the injured or incapacitated. Each group, though working as a cohesive whole, was composed of identifiable individuals with unique personalities — making their cooperation even more remarkable. Both

wolves and humans followed a hierarchical social structure with the leader determined by consensus. Both species adapted to changes in habitat, climate and types of food.

In his remarkable book, *Of Wolves and Men,* Barry Lopez wrote, "Both [species] practiced elaborate ceremonial rituals, gathering and singing before hunting, after eating, or at other occasions ..." Lopez also pointed out the similarities in hunting habits and strategies: both wolves and humans hunted the same prey; both hunted the same ground (territory) repeatedly; both could plan and execute prey drives, ambushes, relay pursuit and encirclement. And, Lopez noted, the territory required to feed a pack of ten wolves was roughly the same size as that needed for a group of 25 people.

Are the similarities between wolves and humans purely co-evolution in action: two intelligent hunters adapting to the challenges and opportunities of an environment? Wolves had evolved as predators in the tundra plains ecosystem, while humans probably began life on the plains as scavengers. It is interesting to speculate whether humans observed the cooperative success of wolves pursuing prey and formed hunting groups in imitation of the wolf packs. Inuit hunters encircle caribou, driving them together before attacking them. Some of their stories say that they began employing this technique only after seeing wolves use it.

At first, there would have been little or no competition between the two groups of predators. Wolves selected vulnerable individuals. Humans, lacking the speed and strength of wolves, used traps, such as pits, or drove herds over cliffs, killing far in excess of their needs. Wolves probably cleaned up the leftovers and may have even followed human hunting parties on the chance of picking up a meal.

Eventually, humans developed weapons that allowed them also to select a specific animal. But unlike wolves, they chose the best of the herd because the meat would be better and more plentiful. Large herds, few hunters and

Wolf Mask, Key Marco, Florida. This mask was found, along with a similar deer mask, carefully wrapped in strips of palmetto leaves. The ears are hinged to allow movement. It is believed to be the work of the now-extinct Calusa people. Material from the site has been dated to about 500–1000 A.D.

primitive weapons meant the long-term effects of removing the best animals from the gene pool were negligible in most places. That situation changed with the advent of modern firearms.

Wolves, on the other hand, are only one power in the long-running "arms race" between predator and prey. As wolves became faster their prey too became faster. Prey formed herds for increased protection, wolves formed packs and developed group hunting tactics. Each shaped the other and continues to do so — when humans allow it.

The skills of a hunting wolf are the stuff of legends. The author of a thirteenth-century bestiary wrote that the wolf's "cunning is such that it does not catch prey near to its lair to feed its young, but fetches it from afar off ... if a twig breaks under its foot and makes a noise, it punishes that foot by biting it."

A Marvelous Hunter Is He
from CYNEGETICA, *a third-century Greek treatise*
on hunting ascribed to Oppian

Fearful is his howl and very high his leap, and he ever shakes his head and his eyes gleam fire ... With much din in early morn he seeks his prey by dawn's first blush, for easily does he feel hunger's pangs ... The lofty hills are his haunt, but when, in winter season, they are mantled in chill snow poured forth from clouds, then the baleful beast, clad in utter shamelessness, comes even unto the city for his sustenance. With stealth and quietness he creeps, so long as he stalks his prey, then suddenly he seizes it in his nimble claws ... Full often the stubborn bronze, full often stone and spear of steel he

The Ainu people of Japan believed that the wolf shared a portion of its kills with humans. They admired the wolf for its ferocity, tenacity and quickness of attack.

breaks amain. He marks the dog-star Seirius [sic] and dreads its rising. Straightway he hides himself in some cleft of the broad earth or some dim-lit cavern until the sun and the star of the ominous Dog abate their scorching heat … A marvelous hunter is he and preys upon the timorous hare, and from his limbs all the hairs bristle and stand out.

Wolves usually locate prey by scent, but may find it by following a track or sometimes just by chance. It takes energy to catch and subdue prey, energy that must be replaced before there is a net gain from the nourishment the prey provides. Being an efficient opportunist, the wolf looks for the easiest possible meal, the one that will take the least energy to acquire. Young animals are easier to kill than adults. Weakened animals tip off wolves to their vulnerability by an unnatural stance, lack of coordination, smell of infection or by other clues not readily apparent to human observers. Once its target is selected, the pack attacks.

Some prey animals, especially healthy adults, will stand their ground and defend themselves. Moose, for example, are strong, ornery and quite capable of killing a wolf. The wolves may press the animal for a few minutes but then leave, seeking an easier victim. Other animals, again usually healthy adults, can outrun pursuing wolves if they are not taken by surprise and get a reasonable head start. Once the pursuing pack realizes it is not closing on their prey, they quickly abandon the chase. The pack may have to test several animals before finding a suitable one.

In a normal attack, the quarry runs, is pursued and caught. Reaching their prey, wolves bite at the animal's rump, flanks and sides, although a smaller animal may have its spine snapped by a single bite. Once the animal is slowed or brought to a halt, wolves grab it by the nose

In nature, death is merely an act in life's drama, and the wolves of Isle Royale perform their appointed role as agents of death for moose, beaver, fox (sometimes), and other wolves (rarely). The wolf itself… most often dances alone with death. Whether it is preferable to be killed or to die by other means is the sort of question that only people ask.

—Rolf O. Peterson, *The Wolves of Isle Royale: A Broken Balance*

or throat and drag it down. Or, if the animal is badly wounded in the initial attack, the hunters may retire a short distance away and await the inevitable death from blood loss and shock. Wolves usually eat the nutrient-rich internal organs first, but may begin gnawing on the rump flesh if the skin has been ripped away during the struggle. Muscle tissue provides the bulk of the meal. Wolves are not dainty eaters — hence the expression "wolfing down one's food." Wolves feeding on a fresh kill tear off great chunks of meat and bolt them down, hide and all. After a meal of caribou, an Alaskan wolf's stomach was found to contain a tongue, liver, windpipe, two kidneys and an ear, as well as hair and large pieces of meat. Unlike herbivores that can graze along at a fairly constant pace, a carnivore's meals often consist of large amounts of food at irregular intervals. If a hunting animal is lucky enough to make a kill, there is always a risk of losing part of the bounty to scavengers or other predators. Being able to gorge quickly when food is available is definitely an advantage, and a wolf may down 20 pounds of meat at a single sitting. No wonder wolves that have recently consumed a kill often lounge in a state of sated somnolence.

The prey a wolf selects depends on its personal taste as well as on what is available where it lives. Although they prefer to kill and eat large ungulates, such as elk, caribou and moose, wolves will make do with what is available. Beaver, berries, waterfowl and carrion may all appear on the menu. They may also ignore their usual fare temporarily to take advantage of a seasonal abundance in the form of spawning salmon or loads of lemmings. Wolves will also eat wolf, probably most often as carrion.

How much meat does a wolf need? According to wolf researcher L. David Mech, an average of about four pounds a day will keep a wolf alive but almost double that is needed if the wolf is to reproduce successfully. The amount varies depending on the physical demands placed on the animal.

The Hopi people of the American Southwest knew from observation that pronghorn antelopes, being the favorite prey of wolves in the region, were very scared of the predator. Hopi hunters used this knowledge to their advantage by building a surround — a corral entered by a chute — and frightening pronghorn into it by encircling them and howling like wolves.

OPPOSITE John James Audubon maintained the image of the fierce predator in his depictions of the black American wolf and the white American wolf.

In Alaska, wolf packs average one kill every seven to 16 days in the summer, but the frequency increased to one kill every five to 11 days in winter. A combination of harsh winter weather and plentiful prey may push a wolf's meat consumption over 18 pounds a day. Dependent young mean more work for a pack. In Wood Buffalo National Park, Alberta, Canada, a pack of eight wolves raising five cubs were recorded as consuming 5570 pounds of edible meat (not total prey weight) between May 1 and October 1.

The relationship between wolves and their prey is a complex subject that has generated a great deal of discussion. In the past, and even today in some places, human hunters concerned with maintaining prey populations for themselves have been quick to lay the blame for any decline in prey numbers on the depredations of wolves. However, determining the exact effect wolves have on prey populations is difficult. Many other factors affect prey numbers.

Lack of forage and harsh weather, especially deep snow, can reduce prey populations. So can killing by other predators, including humans. Lack of alternate prey species may focus the attention of all predators in an area on a single food source. After carefully examining the data from a growing number of studies, many researchers have reached the conclusion that wolves can be a limiting factor — sometimes possibly the controlling factor — of moose, caribou and white-tailed deer populations. But the factors influencing each situation need to be identified and studied before wise management decisions can be made.

Wolf predation influences more than just prey numbers. The results of a four-year study in the Greater Yellowstone area comparing wolf kills and kills made by human hunters showed that carrion from wolf kills is scavenged by more species, contributing to ecosystem diversity. Bald eagles and ravens, both highly mobile, dominated at kills made by humans. The wolf kills are spread out over larger spans of both time and space, allowing broader access.

PLATE LXVII.

CANIS LUPUS, LINN. (VAR ATER.)
BLACK AMERICAN WOLF.
MALE.
½ Natural Size.

White American Wolf

Other recent studies show ecosystem-wide interactions between wolves, browsing animals, such as moose, and tree growth. When the number of wolves on Isle Royale, Michigan, dropped, moose numbers rose. More moose munching reduced the amount of balsam fir growth. It would be interesting to see whether further research — into plants and animals linked to the presence or absence of balsam fir, for example — would reveal an even more encompassing web of interdependence.

Wolves do not always confine their hunting to wild game. When they preyed on our early ancestors' livestock, the human view of wolves' predatory skills began to change from admiration to animosity. However, it wasn't particularly difficult for a skilled hunter-turned-shepherd to defend his flock, and fending off wolves was a normal part of a vigilant herder's job. True burning hatred of the wolf required the fuel of ignorance fanned into flame by fear. As people gradually lost their contact with and knowledge of the wilderness, it became all too easy to replace fact with fevered imaginings.

Fear of the dark and fear of being eaten by a wild animal are innate to the human psyche. Combine the two and you have the beginnings of real terror. Stories of wolves attacking humans come from around the world, as legends and historical fact, but are wolves really a threat to people?

As we have seen, Native North American people who lived side by side with wolves saw them as rescuers. Early trappers told of the ensnared wolf's meekness in accepting its fate. In *Neither God Nor Devil,* Eva Rehnmark writes that a study of European wolf attacks on humans reported between 1815 and 1965 failed to find one that could be verified. A study by explorer Vilhjalmur Stefansson examined global wolf attacks from 1923 to 1936, finding them to be

Why did our ancestors tame and domesticate wolves, of all creatures…? Isn't it strange that, our being such an intelligent primate, we didn't domesticate chimpanzees as companions instead? Why did we choose wolves even though they are strong enough to maim or kill us?

— Wolfgang M. Schleidt and
 Michael D. Shalter, *Co-evolution
 of Humans and Canids*

either completely fictional or extremely exaggerated. The sheer volume of accounts, especially in Europe and Asia, suggests that something was going on, but what? One of the best known and documented cases, the tale of the Beast of Gévaudan, seems to have involved not wolves, but wolf-dog hybrids.

In Vivarais and Gévaudan, France, between 1764 and 1767, two "wolves" killed 64 people and slaughtered a great many domestic livestock before hunters killed them. From descriptions and skull measurements, scientists now believe that the animals, which were much larger than wolves generally found in that area, were not pure wolves but hybrids. They may have been a mixture of wolf and the huge mastiffs that farmers kept as guard dogs.

Rabies lies behind some of the historical accounts of wolf attacks, especially in Europe and Asia. During the Middle Ages, when many tales of the evil wolf appeared, rabies was a common disease in Europe. In 1166 at Carmarthen in Wales, a rabid wolf was said to have bitten 18 people, most of whom later died. Records from eighteenth- and nineteenth-century France list many similar cases. We must remember how terrifying this disease was until Louis Pasteur developed his vaccine in 1885; the only treatment that had any chance of succeeding was cautery. The thought of red-hot iron burning into agonized flesh, and the frightening symptoms of the nearly always fatal disease, fuelled people's terror of wolves.

Confirmed attacks on people by healthy wolves are rare, but they have happened. In 1996, *The New York Times* reported 33 fatal attacks on children as well as 20 other attacks, in the state of Uttar Pradesh, India. Two incidents in Algonquin Park, Ontario, Canada, during the mid to late 1990s involved nonfatal attacks on children. In 2000, a wolf attacked a sleeping kayaker camped on Vargas Island, British Columbia, Canada. It took 50 stitches to close the man's head wound. Wildlife officials could find no reason

for the attack. The only documented human death caused by wolves in North America occurred in 1996 at a private wildlife sanctuary near Haliburton, Ontario. A worker was attacked and killed by five wolves when she tripped and fell in their enclosure. Despite these occurrences, most wolf researchers still believe that, especially in North America, humans have little to fear from healthy wild wolves.

Early engraving showing a settler fighting wolves.

Stories of wolves attacking humans are much more common in Europe and Asia than in North America. One theory about why Old World wolves may have preyed on humans more often than their New World counterparts suggests that wars, and the epidemics that accompanied them, provided Old World wolves with a banquet of dead and dying humans, which gave them a taste for human flesh. And Old World wolves never hungered for long: As the Roman dramatist Plautus (254–184 B.C.) wrote, *Homo homini lupus est,* "Man is a wolf to man."

from **The Blizzard**

Whipped onwards by the North Wind
The air is filled with the dust of driven snow:
The earth is hidden,
The sky is hidden,
All things are hidden —
The air is filled with stinging,
Before, behind, above, below —
Who can turn his face from it...?
All the animals drift mourning, mourning...
Only the Gray Wolf laughs.

Tomorrow three suns will rise, side by side;
All the earth will be covered with dazzling snow —
Cold, cold, and very quiet...
The animals will lie buried in the snow —
Cold, and very quiet...
But the gaunt Gray Wolf will break a new trail,
Running, with three shadows blue upon the snow.

— *Hartley Alexander*

WARRIORS AND WOLVES

A skillful and elusive predator, the wolf has long been a role model and source of spiritual power for warriors. The Vikings wore wolfskins and drank wolf's blood to take on the animal's spirit in battle, while also viewing real wolves as grim battle companions, *hrægifr*, or "corpse trolls," as the Scandinavians called them.

In the New World, the fighters who identified most strongly with the wolf came from nomadic hunting societies, such as the Pawnee and Cheyenne. They emphasized the wolf's predatory stealth and often referred to their wolfskin-wearing scouts as "wolves." War parties sought wolves' help and guidance in locating and attacking the enemy. Warriors used wolf howls for signals and sang wolf songs ending with a lupine cry.

The warriors of many groups belonged to wolf societies. Becoming a member of such a society often involved a ritual transformation from human to wolf. Oglala (Sioux, Lakota) Wolf Society members made spiritually powerful war medicine, and from their ranks came some of the great Native leaders, including Crazy Horse.

In their rituals for drawing upon the wolf's supernatural powers, New World warriors often used wolfskins or other body parts. Some tied wolf hairs to their bandoliers before battle. Others fed their infant sons pieces of wolf heart in the hope that the boys would become brave warriors. Entwining the essence of the predator with the spirit of man: this was the goal of wolflike warriors.

No one can deceive the eyes of a wolf. They always know.

— R. D. Lawrence, *In Praise of Wolves*

The Middle Ages — from about A.D. 500 to 1400 — were a time of fear, chaos and conflict in Europe. As local lords struggled with one another for control, the countryside rang with the crash of arms and the screams of men and horses. Civil wars, royal wars, holy wars — all added to the havoc. Wolves, ravens and eagles, omnipresent scavengers of the bloody countryside, became symbols of battle and its gruesome aftermath:

> "The spear must be seized, morning-cold,
> hefted in hand, on many dark dawns;
> no harp music will wake the warriors,
> but the black raven above doomed men
> shall tell the eagle how he fared at meat
> when with the wolf he stripped the bodies."
> — *from* Beowulf, *tenth-century Anglo-Saxon epic poem*

Sometime in the late eighth century, a new kind of invader stepped ashore in Ireland. For the next few centuries, these raiders brought such terror to coastal areas of Europe that a prayer arose in the lands that fell under their shadow: "From the fury of the Northmen, good Lord deliver us." The Norsemen, commonly referred to as Vikings, came from Denmark, Norway and Sweden. Overpopulation at home and the vulnerability of overseas targets made plundering expeditions attractive. Wealthy men, such as clan heads and land-owning farmers, sought new opportunities for enrichment and exploitation. Poor men looked for a chance to make a living. Together, the two groups formed organized bands of marauders. Skilled sailors, they voyaged south in longboats to attack coastal European targets in hit-and-run raids.

Fierce, brutal and indomitable, the fighting style of the Vikings was that of Odin's warriors, as described by Icelandic historian Snorri Sturluson in the thirteenth-

This sixth-century Viking plate from Torslunda, Sweden, was used in the manufacture of decorative helmet plaques. The figure on the right appears to be a wolf warrior, or *ulfhednar*.

century Ynglinga Saga: "His men went without their mail-coats and were mad as hounds or wolves, bit their shields and were as strong as bears or bulls. They slew men, but neither fire nor iron had effect upon them." This behavior was called "going berserk" (*berserkgangr*). Calling these fighters *berserkr* may have been a reference to their wearing bearskins (*serkr* = shirt) in battle, as some pre-Viking period artifacts seem to show. Credibility is added to this theory by the other name given to them: *ulfhednar*, or wolf-coats. *Hrafnsmál*, a poem written circa 900, describes the cries of the warriors: "The berserks bayed ... the wolf-coats howled." One can imagine the chilling effect of even a few wolf-coats on the ardor of the opposing force.

Warriors of the Viking Age often identified themselves with either the wolf or the bear. The animals represented two different ways of doing battle. Bear was a noble champion, an independent fighter who made his reputation in single-handed combat. Wolf fought as one of a pack, ruthless, cunning and devoted to his comrades — a good description of a Viking raider.

Besides donning a wolfskin, a *berserkr* might prepare for battle by drinking the blood of a wolf or bear. The late twelfth-century historian Saxo Grammaticus described the ritual: "Straight away bring your throat to [the animal's] steaming blood and devour the feast of its body with ravenous jaws. Then new force will enter your frame, an unlooked-for vigor will come to your muscles, accumulation of solid strength soak through every sinew."

Drinking wolf's blood was a way for the warrior to merge his spirit with that of the animal. Wearing a wolfskin served as a reminder of the wolf's power and provided a conduit for it. For men going into a battle that involved face-to-face hacking, horrible wounds and a high probability of dying a painful death, invoking the wolf's spirit provided courage and comfort.

Wolf-coats they are called, those who carry bloodstained swords to battle;
They redden spears when they come to the slaughter, acting together as one.

— from *Hrafnsmál*, tenth-century Norse poem

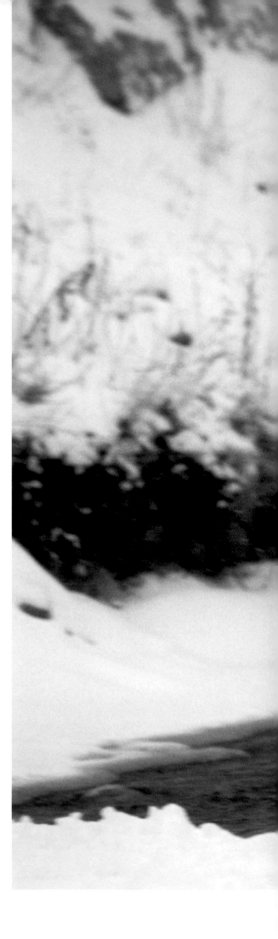

Wolves and Wars at the End of the World

According to Norse mythology, the gods fashioned a magically forged chain to shackle the giant wolf Fenris (also called Fenrir) to the gate of the sunset. To get Fenris to allow the chain to be placed around him, Tyr (also known as Thor) placed a hand in the wolf's mouth as a pledge of good faith. On finding himself bound, Fenris bit off Tyr's hand. *The Edda,* written by Icelandic historian Snorri Sturluson in the thirteenth century, prophesies that after a time of terrible tribulations, the wolf's release from its chain will signal the end of days, the "Doom of the Gods," the Ragnarök.

[First] there shall come that winter which is called the Awful Winter: in that time snow shall drive from all quarters; ... the winds sharp; there shall be no virtue in the sun. Those winters shall proceed three in succession, and no summer between; but first shall come three other winters, such that over all the world there shall be mighty battles. In that time brothers shall slay each other for greed's sake, and none shall spare father or son in manslaughter and in incest; so it says in "Völuspa" [an Icelandic poem from the late tenth century]:

Brothers shall strive and
  slaughter each other;
Own sisters' children shall
  sin together;
Ill days among men, many
  a whoredom:
An axe-age, a sword-age,
  shields shall be cloven;
A wind-age, a wolf age, ere
  the world totters.

Then shall happen what seems great tidings: the Wolf shall swallow the sun; and this shall seem to men a great harm. Then the other wolf shall seize the moon, and he also shall work great ruin; the stars shall vanish from the heavens...Then shall Fenris-Wolf get loose; ...[he] shall advance with gaping mouth, and his lower jaw shall be against the earth, but the upper against heaven ...

Like the Skidi and other Plains Indians, the Absaroke scouts wore wolfskins.

Tsistsistas Wolf Song

SONG OF A TSISTSISTAS (CHEYENNE) SCOUT

TRAVELING IN ENEMY TERRITORY

Wolf I am.
In darkness
in light
wherever I search
wherever I run
wherever I stand
everything
will be good
because Maheo
protects us
Ea ea ea ho.

Nearly all Great Plains cultures linked the concept of a supernatural or ceremonial wolf with the formation and conduct of a war party. Like the Vikings, New World warriors also identified themselves with Wolf but in a different way, emphasizing the animal's stealth rather than its ferocity.

An Oglala man who dreamed of wolves could move toward the enemy's camp like a wolf, so inconspicuously that none would spot him. Red Wing, of the Crow people, declared, "A scout is like a lone wolf that must be looking, looking, looking, all the time." Many Great Plains people called their scouts "wolves" and used the same sign language gesture for both. The lead scout in a Crow war party carried a wolfskin. He might pull the hide up over his head to help camouflage him when spying and, when the weather turned cold, to keep him warm.

The Plains warriors who perhaps most closely identified themselves with the wolf were the Skidi (Skiri) Pawnee. As we learned earlier, the Skidi were called the wolf people, and a wolfskin enclosed their sacred bundle. A true warrior, they believed, followed the ways of the wolf. A Skidi warrior who wished to lead a war party went to the keeper of the sacred bundle and asked to borrow the war clothing it contained. If private assent was given, a public ceremony was held in which the leader formally borrowed war items from the bundle. During this ceremony, the wolfskin from the bundle was prominently displayed to remind the warriors that the wolf was with them. The wolf's powers would also be with them on their journey, present in any objects taken from the bundle. Once the war party formed, it became a society known as *araris taka* — the Society of the White Wolf.

While on reconnaissance, Skidi scouts used wolf cries as signals. Each scout wore two white eagle feathers in his hair arranged so that when he lifted his head above the crest of a hill, the feather tips resembled the ears of a wolf. Wolfskin caps, along with white clay smeared on face and arms, added to the illusion.

An account given in *People of the Sacred Mountain* describes wolves bringing supernatural help in time of war. Around 1830, about half of the Cheyenne people went to attack the Crow to revenge the killing of a Cheyenne council chief. When the Cheyenne located the Crow, they also found Shoshoni camped near by. The Shoshoni joined the Crow and they soon surrounded the Cheyenne. Just as it looked as though all the Cheyenne would be killed, the Sacred Powers sent wolves to give a holy man named Horn, and his son, Box Elder, information about their enemies. Using this knowledge and with the help of the Sacred Powers, the Cheyenne were able to fight their way to freedom. Throughout his life, the spirits continued to communicate with Box Elder through the wolves, who became his instructors. Warriors always wanted to be in Box Elder's war party because he knew through the gift

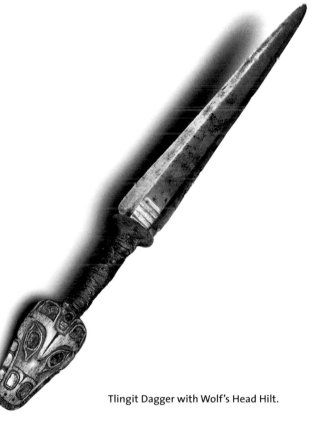

Tlingit Dagger with Wolf's Head Hilt.

of prophecy where the enemy would be and how many of them the Cheyenne would be able to kill.

A Cheyenne warrior named Owl-Man founded a wolf warrior society known as the Bowstrings after receiving supernatural guidance. Caught alone in a prairie blizzard, Owl-Man was near death when he heard a voice directing him to a lodge up ahead. As he sat alone in the empty lodge, Owl-Man heard voices. When he looked outside, there were wolves as far as he could see. He could hear them speaking in his own language, as they approached the lodge. As the wolves passed through the door they became humans. An old Wolf-Man told Owl-Man that the wolves were going to instruct him for the next four days. After that Owl-Man was to return to his people and pass on what he had learned.

The wolf-men, each wearing a wolfskin as a cape with the head on his chest and the tail hanging down his back, danced and sang for four days. Owl-Man learned about three hundred songs, including four war songs. At the end of his stay with the wolf-men, Owl-Man went back to his village and founded the wolf warrior society as he had been instructed.

The Oglala had a society called the *ozunya cin nupa*, which anthropologist Clark Wissler described as a "war shaman wolf cult." A shaman who dreamed of a wolf built a sweat house. Any man who wished could join in the sweat, but if he had slept with a woman the night before, he would go blind upon entering the sweat house. The shaman selected four men and told each to go out, kill a wolf, and have the hide tanned by a virgin. When the wolf hides were brought to him, the shaman performed a ceremony. He attached medicines or powerful charms to each hide, along with an eagle feather and four crow feathers. Below the eyes of the hide, the shaman daubed red paint and he fastened a piece of buckskin painted red to each paw. He sprinkled wild sage on the back half of the hide. Then

The Sign of the Wolf

Noblemen and warriors used wolves as heraldic devices, featuring them in their crests, coats of arms and seals. In England, during the reign of Edward III, Sir Charles Lupus displayed azure wolf heads as part of his Arms. Wolves appeared later on the Arms of Viscount Wolseley, the Lovett family, the Low family and the Lovell family. The wolf can also be seen in heraldry from Scotland, Spain, France, Italy as well as Germany, where it is quite common.

A fifteen-year-old Hunkpapa Lakota (Sioux) boy found a wolf bleeding from two arrow wounds. "Help me," the wolf entreated, "and you shall become great." The boy removed the arrows and cared for the wolf's wounds. As the wolf promised, Sitting Bull (1834–1890) became one of the greatest and wisest of all warriors.

the shaman sang and strange things occurred: whistles made noises by themselves, wolf tracks appeared and the wolf hides moved around. At the conclusion of this ceremony, the shaman announced that the four men who had brought the hides were to go on the warpath.

The men bearing the wolf hides served as scouts for the war party. Each wore his hide on his back, pushing his head through a slit made near the neck. He painted his arms red from the elbows down and did the same to his legs below the knees. Oglala scouts reconnoitered in pairs, only returning to camp when they had spotted the enemy.

Rather than using actual wolf hides, Ponca scouts wrapped themselves in gray or white blankets. Traveling out and back on reconnaissance, they mimicked wolves: trotting in a stooped posture, signaling by howling. If the main body of the war party wanted to recall their scouts, the warriors howled like a pack of wolves.

Warriors also used the wolf's howl in songs. Members of Blackfoot war parties sang wolf songs at night or when the enemy was sighted. These songs could be sung by anyone, not just warriors, to bring good luck and success. Courting Blackfoot sang them to their sweethearts. Each song ended with a howl, symbolizing what the singer hoped to obtain, because the wolf howls when he is hunting.

After their scouts spotted the enemy, Pawnee warriors sang wolf songs during a ceremony held by the war party leaders. These songs derided those who had remained at home or perhaps told of sweethearts. Strangely, a member of a war party could sing about his beloved but he could not speak of a woman or of home, lest he lose his will to fight. Pawnee wolf songs, too, ended with a howl.

The flip side of the warriors' wolf song was observed by George Catlin, an American artist who captured images of the vanishing culture of Native societies. Catlin wrote that Iowa warriors, having kept their whole village awake with "the war dance" for several days, were themselves deprived of a good night's sleep on the night before they left on their raid. After allowing the war party to fall sound asleep, a group of young men gathered and serenaded them with a "curious song, which they have ingeniously taken from the howling of a gang of wolves." The noise continued until the warriors arose, lit a fire and smoked tobacco with their friends, who might stay with them until daybreak. When they left, the serenaders wished the warriors good luck on their quest and a good night's sleep at the end of the coming day.

Ethnologist Frances Densmore, who traveled the western plains from 1911 to 1914 making wax cylinder recordings of Sioux music, captured several wolf songs that told of the loneliness and hardships faced by warriors. Perhaps the most moving was sung by Gray Hawk, an aged Teton Hunkpapa Lakota (Sioux) warrior from the Standing Rock Reservation in South Dakota. Standing Rock was home to Sitting Bull, who was killed there by soldiers in 1890; at the end of that year, Standing Rock people were among those gunned down by the U.S. Army at Wounded Knee. Gray Hawk's song was that of a warrior but it could also be a lament for the Sioux nation.

Beneath all the wolf songs and imitations of wolf behavior flowed a single supernatural current: there is a wolf power or wolf spirit that rules over the acts of war. Preparations for war and war itself had to be conducted in a manner that respected and honored this spirit so that its powers would be used in one's favor. The required ceremonies united the war party, making each warrior one of the pack.

Both Omaha and Hidatsa warriors danced before going to war. Omaha Wolf Society members wore complete wolfskins that had their muzzles painted red. The Hidatsa wolf ceremony, or Tseshatiake, was a demanding ritual that included a four-day fast and self-torture. It ended with a run and a dance that pushed the participants to exhaustion.

Gray Hawk's Lament

A wolf
I considered myself
but
I have eaten nothing,
therefore
from standing

I am tired out.
A wolf
I considered myself
but
the owls are hooting
and
the night I fear.

Sarcee Blackfoot (Tsuu T'ina) wolf tipi, which belonged to Head Chief Big Belly. Blackfoot warriors believed that Wolf could give them unique powers, which brought with them certain obligations.

In several cultures, including many of the Plains groups, the initiation of a young man into a war society involved his transformation into a wolf. In some cases, this was a gradual process without a specific ritual of metamorphosis. Pawnee warriors who had taken part in a war party became part of a somewhat informal wolf society. From time to time, this group held dances in which all young men and boys could take part. In this way, they could learn the rituals, songs and ceremonies necessary for war.

Among the Oglala, the transformation was more explicit. A man who dreamed of wolves or of the Wolf Society viewed it as a sign to join the society. To become a member, he was required to host a feast and then proceed through a set of ceremonies. During his initiation, the prospective member wore wolfskin on his back, arms and legs. On his head he wore a rawhide mask with holes for the eyes and mouth.

Oglala Wolf Society members, who were never numerous, had some power to heal the sick and to remove arrows, but they never treated wounds. They were known for the potent war medicine they made, particularly their powerful lances and shields. In times of trouble, the people turned to the society for guidance. From its members came some of the great Oglala leaders, including American Horse, Crazy Horse, Sword, and Man-Afraid-of-His-Horses.

Initiates became wolves in the Pacific Northwest rituals described earlier. They not only received ideal spiritual qualities for a warrior — bravery and endurance — but some of their training involved exposure to the kind of conditions a warrior might face, such as cold food and cold baths. During the Makah ritual, the initiates used mussel shells to gash their arms and legs in a grid pattern, creating deep bleeding cuts. The scars indicated strength and courage to other members of the order, who knew their source.

In addition to the powers gained from the Klukwalle, a Kwakiutl father who wished his son to become a stealthy warrior would try to obtain other gifts from the wolf. While his son was still quite small, the father killed, or had someone kill, a wolf — an act normally considered wrong. He took the child's hands and placed them on the wolf's front paws, praying "We have come to beg the slyness of your paws, that it may be in this boy's hands." Then the father fed his son four pieces of the wolf's heart, which gave the boy the skill to creep into a house unheard, as a wolf sneaks through a thicket.

Using the wolf's heart in this way is an example of the ancient and widespread practice of sympathetic magic — "like influences like" — which attempted to draw upon an animal's powers through use of its body parts. With the same intent, a Hopi warrior tied wolf hairs into his bandolier. Ghost Head, a Sioux warrior, always took a wolf hide with him on war parties. With the help of the hide, he called upon the wolves for information about the enemy's whereabouts or other important matters.

The desire to tap into the supernatural powers of an admired predator led warriors from cultures as different as Viking and Cheyenne to wear wolfskins. While Old World warriors emphasized the ferocious nature of the animal, New World warriors hoped to acquire its stealth. Warriors on North America's Great Plains, living a nomadic hunting lifestyle similar to that of the wolf, incorporated the animal into many of their war rituals and practices. Becoming a member of a warriors' wolf society meant becoming a wolf, and the metamorphosis could be subtle or dramatic. New World warriors believed that a wolf power ran through the events of war and that this power, like the wolf itself, should be treated with respect.

Two of the decorations on the purse lid from Sutton Hoo, England — site of a Viking ship burial from the early seventh century A.D. — may portray Odin consulting his lupine guardians.

Karok Shaman's Song

I, Wolf of Inam, eat deer, bones and all.
They do not harm me.
You can call on me if you know medicine,
And nothing will harm you.

— *Song sung by a Karok (Karuk)*
shaman to cure a woman with a
bone stuck in her throat.

Shamans and Shapeshifters: Healing and Harming

To ancient people, the spirit world was a source of great power. Shamans, men and women knowledgeable about this other world, sought access to the wolf's spirit and supernatural energy. The Crow and Hidatsa told stories of shamans using wolf powers to heal the wounded and help women in labor. Healers in northern Asia invoked the wolf's assistance, too. Some shamans used the strength they gained from the wolf to cause harm. Shamans often gained their wolf powers in a dream or after being possessed by the wolf's spirit. Some received the powers as a gift after helping a wolf in trouble.

Many cultures believed that wolves — by virtue of their supernatural powers or through consumption of the animal's body parts — could affect the health of man and beast. Wolf liver was prescribed by healers in both pre-Columbian Mexico and Middle Ages Europe. Barren women attended the Roman festival of Lupercalia, named for the legendary nursery cave of Romulus and Remus, in the hopes of becoming fertile. Not all effects were beneficial. Meeting a wolf eye to eye could make a man dumb, and a horse that stepped on a wolf's track would go lame.

We are drawn to wolves because no other animal is so like us... Of all the rest of creation, wolves reflect our own images most dramatically, most realistically, and most intensely.

—Peter Steinhardt, *The Company of Wolves*

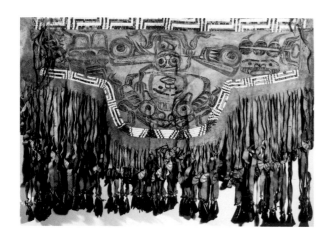

Shaman waist robe.

Without the correct rites and specialized knowledge, gaining access to supernatural power was spiritually and physically dangerous. Men and women who possessed the knowledge for this and other spiritual matters were called shamans, and they were both respected and feared. Among the Kwakiutl, shamans using wolf powers were considered the most powerful of all.

The Crow chief Plenty Coups told of a badly wounded warrior who was carried back to the village after a battle. The man was nearly dead from blood loss when the holy man, Bird Shirt, arrived to help him. Bird Shirt carefully unwrapped the bundle that contained his medicine: a complete wolfskin. The wolf's head was stuffed and portions of its legs had been painted red. The nostrils and a strip below the wolf's eyes were also reddened. Next, Bird Shirt colored himself in imitation of his medicine. As he sang along with the pulsing drums, Bird Shirt painted his shins, forearms, nostrils and the skin below his eyes red. He painted clay over his head to make it look like that of a wolf, and also made clay wolf ears. Bird Shirt imitated a wolf's actions, and he grew increasingly wolflike as he approached the wounded man to begin his healing ritual. The warrior did recover.

Shamans calling on the wolf's spirit to help them heal often employed such evocations of the wolf. A Hidatsa shaman assisting in a difficult birth treated the laboring woman by stroking her back with a wolfskin cap as he sang to the accompaniment of his wolf rattle. Wearing a wolf tail on his head so that the tail flowed down onto his back, a Haida shaman danced around his patient. With his arms and hands he made scooping motions in the air, gathering up the illness and tossing it away.

A Kazan (Volga) Tatar shaman from western Russia treated skin diseases, which were called *bure uy* (wolf's howl), with wolfskins and an imitation of the wolf's howl. A Siberian Yakut (Sakha) shaman wore a green cloth cap with a wolf muzzle sewn onto it, an image of the moon above the muzzle and stars on each side.

Not all used wolf powers to heal. The Bella Coola whispered of a shaman who used a rattle containing a rock crystal when he was healing people. When he wanted to kill someone, he used a rattle that appeared identical but contained human teeth and wolf fangs.

Why did people have such a strong belief in the supernatural powers of animals and the ability of shamans to draw upon them? Most of us live physically separated and insulated from the natural world. But in earlier times, people lived side by side with animals, sharing a world filled with strange and often inexplicable events. These people believed that the barriers between humans and animals, and between this world and the supernatural, were no more substantial than curtains of mist. Shamans knew how to pass through the curtains. They could borrow power from another, take on another's spirit or slip into another's shape.

A shaman might obtain his powers through a spirit quest, as Chilcotin shamans did. They believed that each spirit helper possessed unique skills — the wolf was good at finding lost people. Spirit quests often involved fasting and isolation, creating ideal conditions for communication with the spirits — or for hallucinations, if one rejects the existence of the supernatural.

A Reindeer Chukchee (Chukchi) man, from the northeastern-most part of Siberia, lost sight of the herd he was following and tried to find it again. He spent several months wandering, sometimes going for days without food, shelter or even a fire for warmth. During this time, he encountered animals who played tricks on him. Finally, he met a wolf who shared a reindeer carcass with him. The wolf spoke with the man and later led him to the lost reindeer herd. After this, the man believed himself to be "one with the spirits," although his neighbors ridiculed the idea. More commonly, a shaman on a spirit quest was

How the Shaman Called Fool Got His Powers

The great Kwakiutl shaman, Fool, said that when he was a young man, he helped a wolf who had a bone jammed crosswise in its mouth.

Two years later, he and his family came down with smallpox. The others died and he feared he would, too. Presently he was awakened from sleep by the howling of wolves. Two wolves came to him, vomited foam all over his body and then licked it off. With it, they licked away the scabs and sores caused by the disease. The young man felt himself getting stronger. The wolves kept him warm through the night and repeated their treatment on the next day.

Afterwards, the man was strong enough to stand. As he looked down at the wolves, he recognized one of them as the wolf he had helped before. That night, as the young man slept, he dreamed that a wolf vomited foam onto him and then pressed its nose into his sternum: the wolf was spewing forth magic power and pushing it into the man's body.

The wolf turned into a man and spoke to the dreamer: "Now you will cure the sick, catch the souls of the sick, and be able to throw sickness into anyone among your tribe whom you wish to die."

When the man awoke, the wolves were gone, and he had become a shaman.

—as related by anthropologist Franz Boas

approached by an animal that would speak to him, telling him how to call upon the animal's powers in the future.

Another way to receive lupine powers was to help a wolf in distress. A young Bella Coola woman came across a female wolf struggling to give birth. Something was wrong and the wolf was in great pain. With an evergreen branch in each hand, the woman approached the wolf. Kneeling beside the animal, the woman drew forth four cubs and the afterbirth. In gratitude, the wolf gave her the power of a shaman. Sometime later, the young woman used this power to help another wolf, which was choking on a bone it had swallowed. Reaching into the wolf's mouth, she drew forth the bone and saved the animal's life. Before it trotted away, the wolf gave the woman still more powers.

Some shamans received their powers in a dream. The Kwakiutl shaman Fool dreamed of a wolf pushing its magic into him. In the subarctic, an animal spirit would take control of a shaman while he was dreaming and give him its abilities. The shaman then functioned as a conduit for the spirit, allowing it to visit this world in some disguised form. Perhaps because of the similarity of its lifestyle to that of the subarctic people, the most common shaman spirit in that region appears to have been Wolf. Although the shaman could not control the animal spirit, he or she "became" it. As Norman Bancroft Hunt wrote in *Shamanism in North America*, "'Shaman-as-Wolf' and 'Wolf-as-Shaman' are interchangeable concepts."

Not all spirit possessions happened to shamans or took place peacefully. In 1911 in Greenland, Arctic explorer Peter Freuchen saw a wolf spirit take control of an Eskimo man named Krisuk during an attempt to contact the spirit world. After suffering a seizure, Krisuk stood and howled like a wolf. He began attacking the people near him, who did their best to fend him off and scramble away. As the rest of the village took to their heels in terror, Freuchen wrestled Krisuk to the ground. With amazing strength, Krisuk leapt to his feet, smashed through the igloo wall and raced through the village, howling wildly.

The Copper Eskimos (Copper Inuit), and many other people, believed that a shaman could change his form into that of the animal possessing him, or at least assume some of its characteristics. In animal form, the shapeshifter could visit the spirit world, or use the superior abilities of the animal to travel great distances rapidly in this world. Shamans usually used this ability to gain knowledge with which they helped their people. But shamans were not the only ones who could become wolves — much less benevolent creatures roamed the night.

Among the Navajo (Dineh), two common names for "witch" can be translated as "one who trots along here and there on all fours with it," probably referring to the witch's wolfskin outfit, and simply as "wolf." Anthropologist Clyde Kluckhohn, who interviewed Navajo people between 1923 and 1944, wrote that even the youngest child could tell him about witches taking wolf form to travel quickly at night.

Although rarely seen, Navajo witches could be identified by certain characteristics, as one informant told Kluckhohn: "Magic wolves are about four feet high and four feet long ... tail just hanging down and head is stuffed out with something, and he looks out through the neck. Yes, it is a man dressed in a skin. He looks out through the neck, so if you shoot him in the head it doesn't hurt him." Was it a man-wolf or simply a man wearing a wolfskin? Witches reportedly left behind large wolf tracks. Sometimes a Navajo would shoot a wolf at night and the next day a person would show up with a mysterious wound. Often this person lived far from the scene of the shooting, which could be explained by the witch's ability to travel great distances when in wolf form.

Navajo people believed that a witch would climb up on top of someone's hogan (the roughly circular log

Medicines made from wolf body parts were popular during the Middle Ages as were charms to ward off wolves themselves. This image from a thirteenth-century bestiary shows a man hammering two stones together to keep away the wolf and cubs above him.

OPPOSITE Why are wolves' eyes so like ours? The Bella Coola people of the Pacific Northwest said a shaman was responsible: he attempted to turn wolves into humans but succeeded only with their eyes.

dwellings of the Navajo) and blow "bad witchery," perhaps powder made from a corpse, down the smoke hole. The hogan's inhabitants would suffer bad luck, become very ill or die. Witches were also believed to practice grave robbing, necrophilia, incest and cannibalism. In *Skinwalker*, mystery author Tony Hillerman cast the ancient shadow of the Navajo wolf across a modern New Mexico setting by having one of the villains don a wolfskin to play upon local superstitions, and by including Navajo beliefs about witches.

While shamans and witches called upon the wolf's supernatural powers, others included wolf body parts in their pharmacopoeia. According to Pliny the Elder, a first-century Greek scholar, wolf teeth could be rubbed on the gums of infants to ease the pain of teething. (This remedy was perhaps effective because pressure on the gums often provides relief to teething babies.) Pliny also reported that wolf dung could be used to treat both colic and cataracts.

Wolf liver was one ingredient in an Aztec treatment for melancholia. They also prescribed pricking a dying patient's breast with a sharpened wolf bone to delay death. During the Middle Ages, people used powdered wolf liver to ease the pain of childbirth, and tied a wolf's right front paw around a sore infected throat to reduce the swelling.

If you suffered from insomnia, you might have tried sleeping with a wolf's head under your pillow — the remedy recommended by Sextus Placitus in his *Medicina de quadrupedibus* (*Medicinals from Animals*), written in the fifth century B.C. After a good night's sleep, you could test the ancient Sicilian belief that wearing a wolf's head greatly increased one's courage.

A person bitten by a mad dog could wear a wolf's hide as a charm against rabies. In the Italian province of Girgenti, in Sicily, parents had shoes made of wolf hide for children they wished to grow up brave, aggressive and

Modern Tsimshian (Gitksan) Wolf Headdress created by Walter Harris, 1970.

strong. Bella Coola parents who wanted fierce, intelligent offspring painted a picture of a wolf's gall bladder — believed to be a source of those attributes — on their children's backs.

In ancient Rome, women who longed for children but had none turned for help to a wolf-based ritual. In Act I, Scene 2 of *Julius Caesar*, Shakespeare wrote:

> Forget not in your speed, Antonius,
> To touch Calphurnia; for our elders say
> The barren, touched in this holy chase,
> Shake off their sterile curse.

He was referring to Caesar's barren third wife, Calpurnia, and the festival of Lupercalia held each February. The Lupercal was the cave on the Palatine where a she-wolf was supposed to have suckled Romulus and Remus, which later became a site for fertility worship.

On the day of the festival, goats were sacrificed and their entrails examined for omens. Should the omens be unfavorable, another animal was sacrificed and the process repeated until the signs looked positive. The goats were then butchered, with the best cuts offered to the gods and the rest to the celebrants. Fresh goat hides were fashioned into thong whips called *februa*, or "means of purification," which is where February gets its name. Priests of the Order of Lupercus smeared sacrificial blood on their foreheads with a knife, then wiped it away with wool soaked in milk. Wearing only goatskin and carrying the *februa*, they ran around the edge of the Palatine plateau, striking the women who waited along the route to receive the gift of fertility contained in such a blow.

Not all physical effects derived from the wolf were beneficial. People from many cultures believed that meeting the gaze of a wolf rendered a man speechless unless he spotted the wolf first. Stepping on a dead wolf, said the Bella Coola, caused a person to lose the use of his legs. Pliny the Elder cautioned that a horse stepping on a wolf's track would become lame and ill-winded.

According to Pliny's contemporary and countryman, Plutarch, a wolf's breath was so hot that it softened and melted even the hardest bones. Anything bitten by a wolf decayed with unusual rapidity. Should you choose to eat the meat from a wolf-killed lamb, the Greeks believed you ran a grave risk of becoming a vampire. However, in the Middle Ages, dried wolf meat was eaten as a remedy for sore shins.

❧

Whether as medicinal meat or source of supernatural strength, the wolf played an important role in the beliefs of shamans and healers in many societies. In northern cultures of the Old World and in the New World, shamans drew upon the wolf's power to heal the gravely wounded or to harm an enemy. Some assumed the wolf's shape when they joined with its spirit. A shaman could receive powers in a dream or be given them by the wolf itself in gratitude for a favor. In medieval Europe, where the wolf's supernatural powers were not called upon directly, its body parts were often used to treat illness and disorders. The belief that wolves possessed physical and spiritual qualities that could add to the strengths and abilities of humans reached across time, space and culture.

Wolf is the Zuni Beast God of the East. His power is called upon for the hunt, for war and for curing. Sometimes, he acts as a guardian spirit.

This famous bronze statue now in Rome's Capitoline Museum portrays the wolf suckling Romulus and Remus. The wolf dates from late sixth to early fifth century B.C. The twins were added much later, in the sixteenth century A.D.

He Is What He Is

I have often thought: "Isn't it a pity the old boy can't change his ways so as to be more tolerated by man? But, on the other hand, if he did so, he just would not be a wolf."

—from *The Wolf in North American History* by Stanley Paul Young

PREDATOR BECOMES PREY

Warmer climates at the end of the Ice Age meant changes for wolves and early humans. Wolves followed the herds as they migrated north looking for suitable habitat, while many humans stayed in the south and adopted a settled lifestyle. No longer predatory peers of wolves, these people resented wolf attacks on their newly domesticated livestock. The shift in cultural behavior — from nomadic hunter to settled herder — also transformed the human image of wolves. The wolf became the enemy, hunted with poison and trap.

The battle against wolves was fought with words as well as weapons. From *Aesop's Fables* to *Little Red Riding Hood,* the wolf had a definite public relations problem. Throughout the Middle Ages, the enormously powerful Christian church used the wolf as a symbol of Satan and all things evil. During the same chaotic period, people saw the dark woods around their villages as filled with wolves, outlaws and a terrifying imaginary combination of the two: werewolves.

Today, we may laugh at werewolf stories, but in the Middle Ages hundreds of people were killed because others believed they were werewolves. It was believed that people could become werewolves by deliberately following certain steps or by accidentally doing something wrong. Stories about werewolves existed throughout Europe but were particularly strong and enduring in France.

Its eyes were two gold moons in a stormy sky. There was nothing between us; this void was intimately immense, an interval of alien confrontation.

— Roger Peters, *Dance of the Wolves*

In the New World, until the arrival of the Europeans, things were different. More people remained nomadic hunters and most maintained their respectful relationship with the wolf. Some Native groups killed wolves, while others, such as the Cherokee and Chilcotin, did not. Many northern hunters followed specific rituals before, during and after wolf hunting that would show respect for the wolf's spirit and send it away happy. When North America's Native people hunted wolves, it was usually for their warm fur or for body parts that held the wolf's spirit and power. Their stories emphasize the respect they felt due to the wolf, living or dead.

The relationship between humans and wolves in North America changed drastically with the arrival of the Europeans. At first, settlers killed wolves to protect their livestock and to eliminate competition for deer and other prey. As they moved westward, ranchers and farmers took up the anti-predator battle with increasing ferocity. Soon they had help from federal and state governments. By 1960, wolves had been exterminated from the entire United States except Alaska and northern Minnesota. Today, in areas where wolves are making a comeback, a variety of methods are being used to lessen the conflict between people and wolves and to reduce the number of wolves killed. However, in other parts of their range (notably Alaska), wolves are still being killed in order to increase ungulate populations for the benefit of human hunters, despite serious doubts among scientists about the effectiveness of such programs.

In the 1800s, wolves were trapped for the fur trade, but trapping has declined as pelt prices have fallen. Shooting wolves for sport began in the sixteenth century and held its popularity as the hunters moved from horseback to airplanes and snowmobiles. People can still shoot wolves for fun in Canada and Alaska.

"Beware of false prophets, which come to you in sheep's clothing, but inwardly they are ravening wolves." Matthew 7:15

As the ice retreated for the last time between 20,000 and 10,000 years ago, the herds and the wolves trailing them followed it north. A few groups of humans followed the herds as well, and some of their descendants, such as the Caribou Inuit of central Canada, remained nomadic hunters into modern times. Others changed from hunters to nomadic shepherds, continually on the move with their animals. These early herders probably retained enough hunting skills to successfully defend their small flocks, especially once they began using domesticated wolves (dogs) to help them. Biologist Wolfgang Schleidt suggests that some of these shepherds may have accepted the occasional losses to wolves, which removed the weak and unfit from the herd, as a beneficial form of culling. Of course, not everyone saw it that way and with this fundamental change in human culture — the adoption of a lifestyle sustained by domestic livestock — people and wolves were no longer ecologically compatible.

As Italian zoologist Luigi Boitani points out, we can see the transformation of human attitude clearly when we look at cultures, such as the Lapps (Saami) of Scandinavia, which made the shift from hunting to herding within historic times. As hunters following the reindeer herds, they had great respect for the wolf. Once they domesticated the herds, they referred to it as one of their greatest enemies.

Humans may have adapted to a different lifestyle, but the nature of wolves was unchanged. Finding little dietary difference between a domestic sheep or reindeer and a wild one, wolves naturally preyed upon the easier target. Herders and farmers took a dim view of this opportunistic behavior: the loss of even one animal could be a severe hardship to those struggling to survive.

From this point on, settled humans treated the wolf as a threat and an enemy, beginning a war on wolves in which two separate battles raged side by side: one against the wolf in our mind, the other against the wolf on the land. The hatred engendered by the first caused us to fight the second with relentless fury. The battle that transformed the wolf's image from icon to enemy began rather innocently, with stories meant to teach humans the right way to live.

Aesop's Fables, which date back to around 500 B.C., are some of the earliest examples of animal allegories. In one of the stories, a starving wolf envies a dog's constant supply of food. However, when he learns the dog is chained and cannot run free, the wolf decides the price of comfort is too high. While portraying the wolf as an admirable character here, Aesop also cast him in a far less noble role: in order to snatch a meal from a well-guarded flock, a wolf in another tale finds a flayed sheep carcass and puts on the discarded skin. Now undetectable, he mingles with the sheep and is followed by the lamb whose mother's skin he wears. After dining on this trusting innocent, the wolf goes on to obtain other tasty morsels with little effort.

Cunning, greedy and unscrupulous, this "wolf in sheep's clothing" typifies the tendency of humans to exaggerate and interpret a predator's natural behavior according to our own view of morality. For wolves, more than a millennium of negative propaganda lay ahead.

Medieval Europeans struggled merely to survive and life, especially for peasants, was, in the words of seventeenth-century philosopher Thomas Hobbes, "nasty, brutish, and short." Villages were isolated; the roads were bad and few travelers used them. No one traveled at night or alone through the forests, where wild men and beasts lurked in the gloom.

Medieval custom, language and law coupled outlaws and wolves. When an outlaw fled to escape justice, he put himself outside the protection of the law. He bore a "wolf's head," meaning his value to society was considered to be

A History of *Little Red Riding Hood*

An early French oral folktale, "The False Grandmother," depicts a far different Red than the G-rated heroine we know today. Garbed in a cloak of "harlot scarlet," Red meets a lusty and cunning *bzou,* or werewolf, on her way to grandmother's house. The story was loaded with sexual innuendo. Adults would catch the bawdy references but children would not.

Charles Perrault, who wrote the first published version of the tale in 1697, cleaned it up. However, Red paid the price for bad behavior when the wolf gobbled her up. Some say this tale warned the ladies of Louis XIV's court of the consequences of loose behavior. It was common at the time to say, when a girl lost her virginity, *elle avoit vû le loup*—"she had seen the wolf."

By 1812, when the Brothers Grimm printed their version, the whole thing had been sanitized and moralized to fit an emerging Victorian ideal of what constituted suitable reading for children: disobeying authority has severe consequences; females in distress require a male rescuer. Luckily for Red's self-esteem, later writers gave her the gumption to save herself from the wolf in various ways, including shooting him with a concealed automatic.

The historic versions of Red's tragic tale have been psychoanalyzed with a fine-toothed comb. But no matter how the story changed to reflect society's current view of women, or of morality, one thing remained constant: the wolf represented evil. And in that frozen mind-set lies the true tragedy of *Little Red Riding Hood.*

During the Middle Ages, law, language and custom linked outlaws and wolves.

the same as a wolf's — his death would be beneficial and anyone could slay him with impunity. During the reign of Edward the Confessor, which began in 1042, a condemned criminal was forced to wear a wolf-headed mask and might end his days on the "wolf's-head tree" or gibbet. Sometimes a wolf was hanged beside him. In the eleventh century, Canute the Great decreed that a verwulf, or outlaw, was to be banished "beyond the places where men hunt wolves." In this time of ignorance, superstition and fear, people imagined a hybrid of outlaw and wolf, an evil creature combining the worst traits of each: a werewolf.

Werewolves have a long pedigree, dating back at least to Ancient Greece. A common European werewolf story tells of someone injuring a wolf at night, and a human showing up with an identical injury the next day, very similar to the story about the Navajo wolf. During the Middle Ages, prudent people began concealing scars, in case someone saw them and "remembered" wounding a wolf in the same manner earlier.

People could choose to become werewolves, usually making a pact with the devil in exchange for their powers. They often used a belt of wolfskin or magical herbs to effect the shapeshift. Others became werewolves involuntarily, doing something accidentally to bring about their horrible transformation. Being born on Christmas Eve or drinking water from wolf footprints could both lead to lycanthropy. The medieval belief in werewolves stretched right across Europe into Russia, flourishing during the privations of the Dark Ages and abating slightly when living conditions became less harsh.

During the eleventh and twelfth centuries, a slightly warmer climate and improved agriculture practices brought an end to the Dark Ages. Bountiful harvests allowed the population to grow, providing more laborers and craftsmen. New villages arose, forests were felled for building material and fuel, and roads were cut through some of the remaining stands. Increased hunting and reduced habitat caused the population of real wolves to decline, but the numbers of their allegorical brethren rose dramatically.

The growing presence of the Catholic church permeated people's lives, encouraging them to see God's teachings everywhere. Medieval bestiaries — books containing pictures and moralizing stories about real and imaginary animals — contained dogma cloaked in a veneer of natural history. A stag trampling a snake, for example, symbolized the victory of Christ over Satan. Seeking to use concepts that would have meaning to the common people, the church made heavy use of pastoral imagery: Jesus was the Good Shepherd and the people His flock. Of course, it was easy to cast the role of Satan: "The wolf is the devil, who is always envious of mankind, and continually prowls round the sheepfolds of the Church's believers, to kill their souls and to corrupt them ... Its eyes shine in the night like lanterns because many of the devil's works seem to blind and foolish men like beautiful and wholesome deeds."

Others besides the church used the same technique. In the late twelfth century, Marie de France wrote fables in which wolves stood for greedy nobles who, by failing to behave correctly, caused society's problems.

> The wolf then grabbed the lamb so small,
> Chomped through his neck, extinguished all ...
> They strip them clean of flesh and skin,
> As the wolf did to the lambkin.
> — *Marie de France, writing of the poor's suffering at the*
>   *hands of the rich*

During most of the thirteenth century, Europeans continued to prosper. Life was so good that no one bothered to save for a rainy day. Then it rained.

In this illustration from a thirteenth-century bestiary, a wolf prowls outside a sheepfold just as Satan lurks round the Good Shepherd's flock.

In the late 1200s and early 1300s, the weather was so cold and wet that harvests failed and a series of famines gripped the continent. Those who did not starve to death were easy prey for diseases like influenza and pneumonia. In 1337, the Hundred Years' War began, ravaging the French countryside and providing plenty of carrion for the wolves. Not long after that, things went from bad to worse.

From 1347 to 1351, the Black Plague swept out of Asia and across Europe. More than half the population of Europe died, either from the pestilence itself or from lack of necessities. In villages decimated by disease, wolves fed on corpses that were left unburied because there were not enough healthy people to dig graves. Such macabre scenes haunted survivors and added to the wolf's bad reputation. Belief in the occult and witchcraft rose dramatically as people struggled to understand what was happening in a world filled with death.

Shapeshifting was a common accusation against witches even before the Inquisition began in 1478. During the fifteenth and sixteenth centuries, when the witch-hunting fury reached its peak, the strangest tales were accepted without question. Few had any doubt about the existence of werewolves.

In 1555, Swedish scholar Olaus Magnus wrote that in Prussia, Livonia and Lithuania, on Christmas Eve, "a multitude of wolves transformed from men gather together ... and then spread to rage with wondrous ferocity against human beings and those animals which are not wild." They broke into houses and killed the people within, and vandalized beer cellars by dumping out casks. They stacked the empty casks before they left, Magnus wrote, "thus showing their difference from natural and genuine wolves."

In 1573 near Dôle, France, Gilles Garnier was tried and convicted of killing and partly eating three children

Lon Chaney, Jr., brought the werewolf to the silver screen in *The Wolf Man* (1941) in which a woman recites the famous poem:

Even a man who is pure in heart
And says his prayers by night
May become a wolf when the wolfsbane blooms
And the autumn moon is bright.

OPPOSITE In captivity, a wolf may live to be 13 or 14, but in the wild, a wolf that reaches its fifth birthday has something to celebrate. Disease, starvation and injury take their toll, but by far the greatest killer of wolves is man.

Wolf: a man given to seducing women

——*Oxford English Dictionary*

while he was in the form of a wolf. According to records of the case, one of the most horrifying facts was that although Garnier was in human form when he was caught, he was preparing to eat the body of the boy he had just strangled "notwithstanding it was Friday." On Fridays, of course, the church forbade its followers to eat meat. The black humor of this remark probably never reached Garnier, who was burned alive for his crimes.

Werewolf trials, which can be distinguished in the records from those for witchcraft, led to hundreds of executions during the 1600s. Men, women and children — many of them physically or mentally handicapped — were put to death. The toll was especially high in France. While the trials and killings appear to have stopped by the end of the 1600s, French belief in the werewolf, or *loup-garou*, lingered. In 1927, a policeman from a town near Strasbourg was tried for the shooting death of a boy he believed to be a werewolf. That same year, the last wild wolves in France were killed.

Before Europeans came to the New World, Native people had a respectful relationship with the wolf. Some would kill a wolf while others would not. But few killed it out of fear, and then usually because of apprehension about the wolf's power or spirit, rather than from dread of the animal itself.

The Cherokee, believing a slain wolf's brothers would exact revenge, did not hunt wolves. Any weapon used to kill a wolf, they said, would not work right again. If a wolf was killing livestock, the Cherokee called in a professional wolf hunter who would placate the wolf's spirit and, as an additional safety measure, lay the blame for the wolf's death on another village. The Chilcotin people of British Columbia had a strong taboo against hunting wolves. If a hunter accidentally killed one, he offered apologies. The Ahtna people, who lived in the Canadian Arctic, rarely hunted wolves. They believed that anyone who killed a wolf would starve to death and that special magic was needed to skin a wolf without peril.

People who hunted the wolf used several methods, some dictated by belief. The Comanche people, in a view similar to that of the Cherokees, said that a rifle used to shoot a wolf would never shoot straight again. Only arrows, often tipped with a sharpened wolf's tooth, should be used to kill wolves.

Other hunting methods, such as pitfalls, were practical ways of dealing with a sometimes elusive prey. Arctic people, who were ingenious in their use of limited resources, employed methods that were effective and efficient, even though some seem cruel by modern standards. They dug pitfalls where permafrost allowed, and also built a type of pitfall from ice and snow. They constructed deadfalls using heavy stones and a prop stick baited with fat. When the wolf tugged at the fat, the roof stone fell and stunned or killed it. Perhaps the most common hunting implement was the wolf-killer made of baleen. Strips of baleen with knife-sharp ends were frozen into a lump of fat and left out for the wolves. When a wolf ate this, the fat thawed and the baleen cut through the wolf's

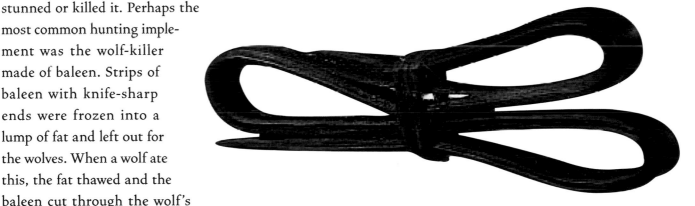

Baleen wolf-killer used by Arctic hunters.

entrails, killing it. A number of variations on this device existed, and those who used it said the wolf usually died very close to the bait site, making recovery easy. Wolf fur was and still is valued by the Inuit for edging the hood of a parka because it does not ice up and become stiff from the wearer's breath.

from **The Trail of the Goldseekers**

O a shadowy beast is the gaunt gray wolf!
And his feet fall soft on a carpet of spines;
Where the night shuts quick and the winds are
   cold
He haunts the deeps of the northern pines.

His eyes are eager, his teeth are keen,
As he slips at night through the bush like a
   snake,
Crouching and cringing, straight into the wind,
To leap with a grin on the fawn in the brake.

He falls like a cat on the mother grouse
Brooding her young in the wind-bent weeds,
Or listens to heed with a start of greed
The bittern booming from river reeds.

He's the symbol of hunger the whole earth
   through,
His spectre sits at the door or cave,
And the homeless hear with a thrill of fear
The sound of his wind-swept voice on the air.

—Hamlin Garland

Northern hunters often practiced special rituals before, during and after wolf hunts. All had to do with respect for their quarry. Among the Inland Eskimos near Icy Cape, Alaska, wolves were taken only for their pelts and their flesh was never eaten. A man who planned on trapping wolves could not cut his hair or drink hot soup for an entire winter. Nor could a hammer be used in his house during hunting season. When he returned home with a fresh wolf pelt, the hunter walked around his house "sun-wise" and kicked the wall several times: four, if the wolf was male; five, if it was female. The kicks signaled the women in the house to bow their heads and turn away from the door. The whole village was alerted and a series of ceremonies to appease and honor the wolf's spirit began. During these rites, which would last for four or five days, depending on the sex of the wolf killed, the hunter could not sleep with his wife and all attending the ceremonies observed a set of food taboos. The hunter's weapons were hung up next to the wolfskin and became the temporary property of the wolf's spirit. Other valuables, such as the women's ulus (knives), were also hung up so that the spirit could take them if it wished. Stories were told to entertain the wolf. On the last morning, the wolf's spirit was sent away as the men cried out, "Leave us like a good soul, like a strong soul." A big feast at the hunter's house ended the ceremonies. During one trapping season, a hunter could take only five wolves and five wolverines. If he left his traps out after that, either he would catch no more or the animals would be angry and kill him for being greedy.

This type of ceremony, which honored the slain animal as a guest and released its spirit, was found in many cultures in strikingly similar form. It was most commonly performed for animals believed to have particularly powerful spirits: bears, wolves and wolverines. The idea was to send the animal's spirit away happy so that it would tell other animals about the good treatment it had received, making them want to be killed by the same hunter. Even among people who had to kill to live, the idea of taking life often brought fear and guilt. Aua, an Iglulik Inuit shaman, explained to anthropologist Knud Rasmussen (1879–1933) that: "the greatest peril of life lies in the fact that human food consists entirely of souls. All the creatures that we have to kill and eat, all those that we have to strike down and destroy to make clothes for ourselves, have souls like we have." Ceremonies of sending away a slain animal's spirit calmed fears of retribution and assuaged guilt by honoring the animal's sacrifice.

Farther south, a story from the Kwakiutl, who rarely killed wolves, describes a much simpler scene that still demonstrates respect. Two men came across the body of a wolf in the woods. Treating the wolf as an honored friend, they wrapped it in a blanket and covered it with rocks. In return, the men asked the wolf to leave behind its luck in the form of a quartz crystal, which they believed every wolf carried in its right shoulder.

On the Great Plains, hunters employed wolf pits covered with grass or branches and baited with buffalo scraps. They often set snares near the trap edge to catch wolves too cautious to be caught in the pit. Deadfalls were used by many people, including the Sarsi (Tsuu T'ina), who traditionally hunted along the Saskatchewan River in Canada. In the winter, Sarsi hunters might hide in a snow bank near the remains of a recently butchered buffalo and wait for wolves to come and feed on the leftovers.

Although some Native people, such as the Arikara, Mandan and Cheyenne, occasionally killed wolves for food, most killed them for their pelts. Besides their practical value as warm fur, the skins carried the spirit and power of the wolf. Whether they killed wolves for food or fur, before the coming of the Europeans, the people of North America never killed enough to have an impact on the population. This was due to three simple facts: there were relatively few

Tlingit Dance Hat representing wolf's head with killer whale dorsal fin. The two species were believed to be able to transform into one another. This hat was worn at potlatch dances by a member of the wolf clan.

Wolves and Predator Control

ca. 800 Charlemagne founds special wolf hunting force, the Louveterie, which remains active until 1789. It is reactivated in 1814 and the last French wolves are killed in 1927

985 Britain's King Edgar imposes annual tax of 300 wolfskins on Wales; Welsh wolf population quickly exterminated

1500 Last wolf killed in England

1609 Cattle, pigs and horses arrive in Jamestown, one of the first English colonies

1630 Wolf bounties established in Massachusetts

ca. 1684 Wolves extirpated in Scotland

ca. 1770 Ireland's last wolf killed

1772 Denmark's last wolf killed

1817 More than 1000 wolves killed in Prussia

ca. 1870 Livestock raising moves into the rangelands west of the Great Plains

1883-1918 More than 80,000 wolves killed in Montana for bounty

1915 U.S. federal government enacts wolf eradication program for western states

1943 Last wolf killed in Yellowstone

1945 Wolves extirpated in lower 48 U. S. states except for small population in northern Minnesota and on Isle Royale in Lake Superior

people spread out over a great expanse; there were many, many wolves; and there were no firearms.

Throughout the history of civilization, right into our own time, wolves have been hunted with a vengeance seldom seen against any other animal. The hatred and fear some people felt toward these animals led to cruel and gruesome acts when they were captured. After describing a particularly hideous torture, one writer concluded "Such methods may seem cruel, but the wolf itself is a cruel beast and could scarcely expect to be treated better." These words are not from a medieval treatise written at the height of the werewolf scare, but from a "factual" book on wolves written in 1964! The same book included dramatized accounts of wolf attacks and described wolves as "essentially cowards at heart," "savage beasts" with "cruel eyes." Looking beyond the hate, one sees that wolves are killed for one of three sometimes overlapping reasons: for predator control, for fur and for sport.

In Europe, wolves were killed because they preyed on livestock, on game animals that humans wanted to kill themselves, or on people. Traps, poison and eventually firearms were used to exterminate wolves across wide areas. Some scattered packs managed to survive in mountainous areas on the continent.

Immigrants to the New World brought their ideas about wolves with them. Wolf researcher Luigi Boitani writes that to the European settlers of America, the wolf "was the essence of wildness and cruel predation, the ally of barbaric Indians, a creature of twilight. Its elimination was depicted as more than just practical; it tested the resolve and spiritual fortitude of the community."

Early settlers killed wolves not just to protect themselves and their livestock from a perceived threat; they killed wolves to eliminate competition. Deer and other ungulates were an important source of food, clothing and income for pioneers. People relied on deer for meat and

clothing, bringing in domestic livestock later. Deerskin became a valuable export: 30,000 skins were shipped to Europe in 1753 from North Carolina alone.

By the mid-1700s, deer, bison, elk, moose, woodland caribou and beaver — prey favored by settlers, Natives and wolves — existed in very limited numbers or were completely absent from colonized areas. Overhunting seems to be the main reason for this loss, although habitat destruction certainly contributed . Gaunt, hungry wolves deprived of their natural prey turned to livestock. This pattern occurred over and over as each new wave of settlement pushed farther west.

When sheep and cattle arrived on the rangelands, the battle against the wolf reached a fever pitch. Poison and traps proved effective against wolves, though they killed large numbers of other animals as well. The United States government took over the wolf control program in 1915, but by that time it was merely a mopping-up operation. Except for a small population in Minnesota, wolves were gone from the lower 48 states.

In the United States today, livestock depredation is usually dealt with on a case-by-case basis. The offending wolf may be killed or relocated. In Minnesota, selective removal of wolves preying on livestock and payment of compensation to the farmer is reducing the livestock-wolf conflict, and encouraging acceptance of wolf recovery.

Other states also have compensation programs, and a compensation fund managed by the private group Defenders of Wildlife allows wolf lovers to put their money where their heart is. Between 1987 and 2001, the fund paid livestock producers in Montana, Idaho and Wyoming a total of $150,000 for confirmed or "extremely probable" wolf-caused losses. The payments have increased support for wolf reintroduction in these states. In Europe, compensation programs are run by some governments — including those in Romania, Croatia, Norway, Spain, Portugal,

A wolf pack's territory may encompass tens, hundreds or thousands of square miles, depending on the density of prey and the size of the pack.

France, Poland and Italy — and by private insurance companies. However, to be effective and to avoid creating a situation of economic dependence for the livestock owner, any compensation program needs to be combined with prevention.

A variety of methods has been used to keep wolves from killing livestock. Sheep and goats, more vulnerable to attack than cattle, are probably best protected by the presence of an alert shepherd and guard dogs. Bringing livestock into an enclosure at night is also effective. Harassment and relocation of problem wolves, electric fences, aversive conditioning using bad-tasting substances on carcasses, and disruptive stimuli, such as loud noises and flashing lights, have all been tried with varying degrees of success. While llamas and donkeys have proved successful in guarding flocks against coyotes, they do not seem to be much of a deterrent to wolves.

Changing the way livestock is managed can also reduce losses. A study initiated and funded in part by the Nez Perce tribe showed that wolves killed calves that were of lowest weight, least protected by people and closest to an active wolf den and forest cover. In other words, the wolves were treating the cattle just as they would wild prey, observing the herd and choosing the easiest targets. Livestock managers can provide less tempting opportunities by moving animals to pastures away from wolf dens, by having calving and lambing take place in protected conditions near inhabited areas, and by allowing the calves and lambs to gain some size before turning them out to pasture.

No single measure will solve the problem of wolf depredation on livestock. Individual situations require unique solutions. Financial, logistical and cultural considerations all play a part in what type of wolf control is used in a particular area. Some livestock owners, particularly in poorer parts of Europe, cannot afford electric fences to protect their animals. Others cannot obtain the materials needed

A striking brooch/pendant by Haida artist Bill Reid portrays the mythical sea wolf.

for a particular strategy or do not wish to change from the way things have always been. These factors need to be taken into account when alternatives to lethal predator control are proposed.

In the United States, Defenders of Wildlife is addressing the predator control situation with actions as well as words. Besides making loss compensation payments, Defenders uses its Bailey Wildlife Foundation Proactive Carnivore Conservation Fund to purchase regular and electric fencing, guardian dogs and other protective materials. Defenders also funded aerial monitoring to obtain information about wolves in Wisconsin and conducted workshops on protecting domestic sheep from wolves. These actions show livestock owners that wolf supporters are willing to share the costs of having wolves around, which makes nonlethal control more attractive. In some situations, however, lethal measures are still considered the best option.

Just as settlers killed wolves to reduce competition for deer, wolf control programs are now being used to increase ungulate populations for the enjoyment of human hunters. Today, most hunters are out for sport; even when they use the meat and hide, only a small percentage rely on what they kill for subsistence. In some areas, such as parts of Alaska, sport hunters provide revenue to the tourist industry and to the government; maintaining enough game for them to kill is an important economic consideration.

Predators can certainly lower ungulate populations, especially when they take large numbers of caribou or moose calves from a population already under pressure. But does removing wolves increase the game population? Sometimes yes, sometimes no. Research in British Columbia and the Yukon shows that in some cases killing wolves does result in higher survival rates for moose and caribou calves. However, out of 11 tests of wolf control in Alaska, only three resulted in increased game numbers.

The wolf's brain, weight for weight, is one-third larger on average than that of the domestic dog, and from this we would suppose a higher degree of intellectual development. One may suggest that, apart from the higher primates, the wolves are the most intelligent of terrestrial mammals. It is sad that this splendid creature should have become pitted against man in an age-long struggle for superiority.

—Richard Fiennes, *The Order of Wolves*

Another problem with wolf control as a game management strategy is that the effects do not persist once the killing stops. In Canada and Alaska, researchers found ungulate mortality rates returned to what they had been before the control program started. This is not due simply to wolves coming in from outside the control area.

Consisting of highly adaptable and fertile animals, wolf populations are amazingly resilient. Research indicates that from 28 to 50 percent, or even more, of the fall wolf population in a given area must be killed to prevent them from being able to replenish their numbers — not just once, but year after year. Even if killing that many wolves were practical, it would certainly be controversial.

Killing wolves can be a short-term solution to protect livestock or to increase a targeted ungulate population, but it is costly in terms of both money and public harmony. It is clear that lethal wolf control should be a last alternative, undertaken only when other measures fail and scientific evidence demonstrates its necessity.

In the mid-1800s, the fur trade provided another reason for killing wolves. Sewell Newhouse's steel leg-hold trap, a vast improvement over its predecessors, provided an efficient way to take wolves without damaging their pelts. Although many early sales of wolfskins were made to Europe and Russia, wearing wolf fur never really caught on in Europe.

Today, not many trappers go after the wolf. Pelt prices often do not leave much profit, considering the costs involved in obtaining the wolfskin. In Arctic Native communities, wolf hides are part of a traditional economy, although the methods used to obtain them are usually quite modern. In Alaska, the only U.S. state that allows wolf trapping, there are no limits on how many wolves each trapper can take. In Canada, trapping is permitted in all provinces at certain times of the year and year-round in Ontario. Limits vary by province. In Europe and Asia,

In their continual search for food, wolves can lope along at 5 to 6 miles per hour for several hours. They may travel 15 to 40 miles in a single night. Individual wolves have covered 1600 miles in a year.

wolves are trapped in several countries including Romania, China and Russia.

Not all wolfskins that find their way to market are supplied by trappers. Shooting wolves for sport began in Europe as far back as the sixteenth century, when people accumulated enough wealth to have leisure time. It was a popular entertainment for eighteenth-century European gentlemen and also with North Americans in the 1800s. On the Great Plains, wolf hunts were a common weekend event in the early 1900s. After World War II, wolf hunting as sport took a leap in popularity. About that time, hunters started shooting wolves from airplanes, a "sport" that continued into the 1970s. Snowmobiles came on the scene in the 1960s, giving hunters a chance to chase down wolves before shooting them and allowing access to areas rarely hunted before. The most distasteful practices were eventually banned, thanks to the outcry from wildlife advocates and from ethical hunters who respect the animals they pursue, believe in the concept of "fair chase," and seek to minimize their quarry's suffering.

People can still hunt wolves in Alaska and Canada, but the use of airplanes, snowmobiles and vehicles during the hunt is strictly regulated and in some cases forbidden altogether. Annual and daily bag limits apply in most places, although once again Alaska has no limit on the number of wolves that can be killed in areas where hunting them is allowed. With proper management, wolves are a renewable resource capable of generating income. Whether killing them for entertainment is the right way to use that resource is a topic for debate.

Today, wolves have been reintroduced in some areas of the United States and the existing populations are expanding. The European populations, too, are slowly making a comeback. In these places, depredation payments are helping to decrease human animosity toward their renewed presence. In many areas, nonlethal predator control strategies are gaining broader acceptance but wolves are still being killed to protect livestock and to increase game populations for human hunters. Wolves are also trapped for fur and shot for sport in parts of their present range. Wherever they are found, wolves still provoke reactions stemming more from fear than fact, and the desirability of their presence is often the subject of heated arguments.

A great deal of heat and not much light — discussions about wolves often resemble that long ago fire where this story began. After so many centuries together, many filled with fear and hatred on our part, where does the human–wolf relationship stand now? And, more importantly, where do we go from here?

Bella Bella (Heiltsuk) carved and painted red cedar sitting wolf.

A Blessing Be Upon Us All

We ask the Creator that wolves may be allowed to run free again, that they be able to live, to be a part of us, to be a part of our land, to be a part of the creation for which they were intended.

— *Blessing by Nez Perce elder Horace Axtell at a ceremony celebrating the return of wolves to Idaho*

AT THE EDGE AGAIN

Wolves are still wolves, but recently our view of them has changed yet again. For many, they have become the icon of wilderness. They are still a symbol of what lies outside the boundaries of civilization but, in a world rapidly filling with pavement and people, their wildness is now desirable rather than threatening. However, if we have learned anything from studying the past, it is that we should take images and icons of wolves with a healthy dose of skepticism. Wolves are no more spiritual, peaceful guardians of the wild than they are evil minions of Satan: they are simply wolves, remarkable and beautiful enough in and of themselves. Although having a positive image of wolves may make it easier for people to accept their presence, we must understand the true nature of the wolf when we make decisions on how to manage wolf populations.

In considering this crucial task, it is important that any decisions are based on science, not emotion. There are many areas of interest, such as the ripple effects wolves may have on their environment, that need more investigation, but only science can provide the foundation for discussion and for sound management practices. Whatever choices we make with regard to the wolf will have lasting effects, including some that are subtle but significant.

The reintroduction of wolves to the Greater Yellowstone Ecosystem was a triumph brought about by people with many different interests working together. Communication, although sometimes carried out

The wolf was once widely seen as a symbol of the depravity of wildness; it is now to many a symbol of the nobility of nature. Largely by the use of symbols, we nearly eradicated the wolf. Largely by manipulating symbols, we may yet save it.

— Peter Steinhart, *The Company of Wolves*

153

at rather high decibel levels, eventually carried the day. Successful reintroductions bring their own set of problems, however, such as how to deal with expanding populations. Wolves need a great deal of space and, like many other species, are threatened in many places by the fragmentation of their habitat into small, isolated islands of wilderness. Humans have applied terrible pressures to wolf populations but their adaptability and resilience have served them well and will continue to do so, with human support.

Although much reduced from its former extent, the range of the gray wolf today includes North America, Eurasia and the Middle East. Alaska's wolf population is believed to be between 5900 and 7200. In Canada, a stronghold for the species, approximately 50,000 to 60,000 wolves roam over 80 percent of their historic range. South of the Canadian border, about 750 gray wolves live in the northern Rocky Mountains of Montana, Idaho and Wyoming. Wolves are also reappearing in places from which they had been exterminated.

In Minnesota, wolf populations have climbed from extremely low numbers in the 1960s to about 2500 living in the wild today. The wolves' range has expanded westward and southward to cover nearly half the state. Residents living in the suburbs of Minneapolis and St. Paul occasionally hear a wolf howling. In Wisconsin and the upper peninsula of Michigan, too, the wolves are back.

The largest existing population of wild gray wolves makes its home in the countries of the former Soviet Union. In 1999, Russia and other former Soviet republics reported stable or increasing wolf populations. However, most of the region has been suffering through severe economic decline and social upheaval. Increasing poverty has pushed more people into relying on natural resources for subsistence, and poaching has increased significantly. Populations of game species, food for wolves as well as humans, have declined sharply in many areas. Habitat destruction and a decrease in the numbers of domestic livestock have also reduced the wolves' prey base. Information from Kyrgyzstan, where pressure is increasing to reinstitute wolf control programs, indicates that the real status of wolf populations in the former Soviet Union needs investigation.

Europe's gray wolves live in small, isolated groups forming a highly fragmented population. Although Poland's total wolf population is estimated to be only 600 to 700 animals, the thickly wooded slopes of the Bieszczady Mountains are believed to be home to the highest density of wolves in Europe: about 4.2 wolves per 40 square miles, according to researcher Wojciech Smietana (nine wolves per 40 square miles, according to government data). Wolves inside the 104-square-mile Bieszczady National Park gained legal protection in 1973. However, until 1998 they were still hunted inside the park. Today, illegal hunting and a dramatic decline in the numbers of red deer, the wolf's main prey species, continue to threaten Bieszczady's wolves.

Polish wolves may be recolonizing areas from which the species was extirpated. In 2003, a gray wolf pack was spotted in German forests near the Polish border for the first time in more than 150 years. Until 1990, German and Polish laws required people to kill any wolves they saw in the area. Growing concern for the environment and increased understanding about the part wolves play in maintaining a healthy ecosystem have created a more welcoming attitude among area residents and government officials. Placing their faith in deterrent measures, including electric fences, even the German sheep breeders' association is supporting the wolves' return.

In northern Europe, where one might expect to find gray wolves enjoying a favorable habitat as they do in North America, wolf numbers are low. There is little open wilderness. Wolves hunting for food not only compete with

Nazis and Wolves

Adolph Hitler, who was enthralled by Germanic legends and stories of the supernatural, had a special fascination with wolves and their predatory image. He sometimes used "Herr Wolf" or "Conductor Wolf" as an alias. "Wolf's Gulch" (*Wolfschlucht*), "Wolf's Lair" (*Wolfschanze*) and "Werewolf" (*Wehrwolf*) were code names for various military headquarters. The Nazis, drawing on the works of philosophers Friedrich Nietzsche and Oswald Spengler, believed predators lived closer to nature, possessing more vigor and virility than the creatures upon which they preyed.

In 1934, Germany placed the wolf under protection, becoming the first nation to do so in modern times. This was, however, a tribute to the iconic wolf rather than the actual predator: the last wolves in Germany had been killed around the middle of the nineteenth century.

Nietzsche, Spengler and others made their case for noble predators after the real wolf and its perceived threats vanished. Nazis glorifying the wolf did not have to deal with farmers worried about their livestock.

other predators but use the same habitat as hunting, grazing and logging interests. Despite these challenges, wolves have begun to make a comeback in some places. Sweden, where wolves were considered extinct in the 1960s, may have over 100 now. Finland also has approximately 100 wolves, while Norway is home to probably ten or fewer. However, support for continued growth of Scandinavian wolf populations is far from widespread. Wolves find easy prey among reindeer herds, crucial to the existence of the nomadic Saami people in northern Scandinavia and Russia, and in sheep flocks, common in parts of Norway and Sweden.

A 1996–97 white paper (Report No. 35) set out the Norwegian government's official position: they wish to maintain viable populations of large predators including wolves, have international obligations to do so, and therefore must take steps to reduce conflicts between livestock and large predators. Despite this official stand, in response to the concern of sheep farmers, Norway killed 26 wolves from 2000 to 2002. The current management strategy is to give priority to livestock interests in some areas and predators in others, which seems unlikely to work for wolves, given their wide-ranging, opportunistic nature.

One of the last places most people would think to look for wild wolves is in Italy, a country with an average of 500 people per square mile. In some areas of Canada, wolves clear out when the human population rises above three people per square mile, but some Italian wolves live less than 16 miles from Rome. The country's total wolf population has grown from about 100 animals in the 1970s to around 500 today, thanks to a fortuitous combination of events.

In 1971, Italy's wolves received full legal protection. At about the same time, large numbers of farmers began moving to the cities. Woodlands reclaimed abandoned fields, and wolf habitat increased. Hunters reintroduced

"See me for what I am, not as you wish to use me," is the silent cry of wilderness, of wolf, whale, forest, and ocean alike.

— Michael W. Fox, *The Soul of the Wolf*

species including wild boar and roe deer to the woods, providing a prey base. All is not sweetness and light for Italy's wolves, however. Each year, poachers claim about 20 percent of the population.

In the late 1960s, Spain's wolf population consisted of only about 400 animals. Today, it is estimated at between 1500 and 2500 wolves — the largest population in Western Europe. Not everyone is happy to see wolves again. Farmers who had grown accustomed to leaving livestock unprotected suffered heavy depredation, and many older residents feel lingering hostility from past incidents. Protective measures have helped to reduce the number of attacks but Spanish wolves are still being shot, legally and illegally. On the black market, a wolf's head brings a good sum.

Poaching is rampant in Europe and probably is the greatest cause of mortality for wolves there, but wolves are killed illegally in North America, too. In 2003, out of five wolves found dead in the Yellowstone area, only one died of natural causes: three were shot and the collar of one wolf was found transmitting a signal from beneath the water near a dam.

Despite the threats of poaching, habitat destruction, and human encroachment, wolves are doing better in many locations thanks to new attitudes and new management strategies. Nonlethal predator control measures combined with well-thought-out predation compensation schemes are encouraging even those with livestock at stake to consider the possibility of wolves as neighbors.

"Wilderness without animals is dead. Animals without wilderness are a closed book."

— Lois Crisler, quoted by Peter Steinhart, *The Company of Wolves*

...next in rank stood the male gray wolf, whose cry,
Though uttered without effort, verily made the earth
   to tremble,
Even the stable earth to tremble,
Such shall be the legend of the people.

— from Omaha ritual of the cosmic forces

Communication among all stakeholders is crucial when deciding management strategies for wolves. With discussion, unlikely allies like hunting groups and wolf supporters may come to realize that they share common ground. Wolves are a keystone species whose presence affects many other plants and animals. Habitat set aside for wolves is also available for elk, moose and other big game, as well as for all other living things in their ecosystem. The foundation for discussions — and the bedrock upon which all sound wolf management must be based — is science.

Science opens our eyes to the reality of wolves' lives: how many there are, what they eat, where they travel, how much space they need to thrive and reproduce. This information should be used to adjust management strategies. For example, wolves in Yellowstone Park and people who hunt just outside the park both show a preference for cow elk in midwinter. A reduction in cows taken by hunters at this time of year may be necessary for the long-term health of the elk population.

Of course, there are gaps in our knowledge of wolves. More research is needed in several areas, including the relationship between wolves and domestic livestock. The role of wolves as a top-level predator in complex ecosystems — rather than just how their relationship with prey could affect humans hunting the same quarry — should also be investigated. Not every aspect of wolves' interactions with their environment can be studied or quantified, but the more information we have, the greater our chances of making wise choices.

Some effects of our historic treatment of wolves, such as their absence throughout much of the lower 48 U.S. states, are obvious. But others, such as the nature of the wolf photographs in this book and in the vast majority of other wolf books and calendars, are apparent only to a knowledgeable observer. Wolves are wary by nature and where they are hunted by humans even more so. They are also highly mobile, hard to find and not particularly numerous. Add to these difficulties the fact that no ethical photographer would want to cause stress to an animal or endanger himself by getting too close. How, then, are all these wonderful photographs of wolves obtained? The answer is, by working with animals raised by humans and habituated to their presence.

Wolves born and raised in captivity have been a photographic and cinematic staple for many years. Some photographers have been open about where the images came from but many have preferred to keep this information quiet. Working with captive animals allows photographers to show the details of wolves and their lives — even something as intimate as giving birth — which would be impossible in the wild.

The life of a wolf, or any predator for that matter, is a hard one. Parasites, injury and disease all take their toll, and wild wolves are seldom as flawless as the ones that grace the pages of magazines, calendars and books. Captive wolves have played a huge role in sharing the beauty and spirit of the species with millions of people, thereby attracting their attention to the welfare of wolves and the wilderness. There is a touch of surrealism in the knowledge that, without photographs of captive wolves to stir the public imagination, there almost certainly would be no wild wolves running free in Yellowstone today.

The successful reintroduction of wolves to Yellowstone National Park is a shining example of what is possible when interested parties work together. The last Yellowstone wolves were exterminated in the 1920s. In the decades that followed, attitudes changed and national parks came to be viewed not as amusement parks for humans but as havens for endangered species. Still, from concept to conclusion, it took almost 20 years of heated debate among a variety of interested parties —

A Success Story

The reintroduction of gray wolves to the northern Rocky Mountains is one of the greatest conservation stories of all time. But it took a federal court to ensure a happy ending for all gray wolves.

In 2002, northern Rocky Mountain wolves had reached the recovery goal set for them under the Endangered Species Act (ESA) of "30 breeding pairs of wolves well distributed through the 3 states of Idaho, Montana and Wyoming for 3 consecutive years."

Because of this success, the U.S. Fish and Wildlife Service issued the Wolf Reclassification Rule which downlisted wolves from "endangered" to "threatened." Delisting the wolf from the endangered list meant an end to recovery planning throughout the United States.

Along with four coalition partners, the National Wildlife Federation challenged the legality of the Wolf Reclassification Rule. On January 31, 2005, a federal district court ruled that the USFWS violated the ESA when it reduced protections for gray wolves across most of the lower 48 United States. The gray wolf is back under the full protection of the ESA and the government must continue wolf recovery efforts throughout the species historic range.

the Environmental Impact Statement for the wolf reintroduction project included 160,000 comments by the public — before wolves returned to Yellowstone. In 1995 and 1996, 31 Canadian wolves were released in the park. By 2003, there were 148 wolves in 14 packs living in the park itself, and about 271 wolves in the Greater Yellowstone Ecosystem, which also includes areas adjacent to the park in Montana and Wyoming.

Aside from the direct effect on prey animals, the presence of the wolves has changed Yellowstone in several ways. Some far-reaching ecological impacts may take decades to become evident but already there appears to be a change in vegetation type and growth in some areas. When there were no wolves to worry about, elk herds browsed along streams in the winter, killing off young cottonwoods, willows and berry-producing shrubs. This endangered the whole streamside ecosystem and, with no young trees replacing those that died, it appeared the cottonwoods of Yellowstone were headed for oblivion. Since the return of the wolves, young cottonwoods and other streamside shrubs are becoming more numerous and taller in areas where the elk feel unsafe. Scientists are hoping to see a similar effect on aspens, which also suffer from over-browsing.

Bringing the wolves back to Yellowstone has also changed the focus of many visitors to the park. "The great, unanticipated thing is the joy the public has gotten out of the wolves," says Yellowstone Wolf Project Leader Doug Smith. On November 5, 2003, park officials marked the thousandth consecutive day that someone spotted a wolf in the park. Prior to the reintroduction, scientists and planners felt the wolves would be shy and difficult to find. Now considered one of the best places in the world to view free-ranging, wild wolves, the park is a mecca for wolf enthusiasts. Most glimpse the wolves at a distance, but sometimes the wolves come near roads. Park officials worry about the

wolves becoming habituated to humans and urge excited wolf-watchers to keep their distance. "Undisturbed space is among the greatest of their needs," reminded the park's thousandth-day announcement. "Respect this and you will be rewarded by seeing more of their natural activities and seeing how they live in the wild."

In 1995, wolves were also reintroduced into Idaho. The United States Fish and Wildlife Service (USFWS) released 15 individuals that year and an additional 20 the following year. Working with the Nez Perce Tribe, the USFWS monitored and managed the recovery program. As of 2003, there were approximately 362 wolves in 41 packs with 25 breeding pairs spread from the Canadian border to near the southern edge of the state.

Successful wolf populations can create their own problems. A fierce debate is currently raging in the United States about whether wolves have recovered enough to be removed from the protection of the Endangered Species Act. In Minnesota, wildlife managers and residents are having to come to terms with the harsh reality of controlling the burgeoning wolf population. In order to reduce dispersion and minimize contact with humans, David Mech estimates that 300 to 500 wolves will need to be killed each year. This is not news that those who love the wolf want to hear, but it is a part of dealing with real wolves in today's world.

Wolves today face different challenges than their ancestors did. But like their ancestors they are adaptable, clever and capable of cooperative effort. Given certain minimum requirements they will continue to exist. However, existence of individuals and survival of an evolving species are two different things.

If we preserve only islands of habitat separated by large unprotected areas, we may be condemning wolves and other species to death despite our best intentions. Without access to other populations, isolated packs will become genetically uniform. Genetic diversity provides the raw material for evolution and, ultimately, survival. Joining existing refuges with wildlife corridors, and setting aside wildlife areas large enough to allow the existence of genetically healthy populations, are two important steps toward ensuring the future of wolves and other species, and toward enhancing our own.

When our lifestyle was closer to that of the wolf, we made it a hero and a legend. Hunters and warriors admired and praised a kindred spirit. When our life turned from predatory to pastoral, the wolf became our enemy. With poison and pen, tale and trap, we drove the wolf from our lands and our hearts. Now, as we stand on the verge of losing so much of what we hold in trust for future generations, we turn again to the wolf, making it a symbol of hope. We are nearing completion of a circle that will either enfold humans with all other living things on this planet or isolate us forever from the gift of their presence.

For early humans, a circle of firelight formed a safe haven from creatures that roamed the surrounding darkness. Now we must use the light of wonder and knowledge to create a refuge for wolves and other animals by preserving the wild places they need to survive. My hope is that people sitting by a fire on some far-future starry night may be touched by an ancient message from the darkness — the wild, haunting howl of a wolf.

Japanese Netsuke Depicting Wolf.

APPENDIX: *Members of the Pack*

This information about wolves and wolflike canids comes from many sources, including Defenders of Wildlife, 2003, IUCN, 2003, Macdonald, 2001, Paquet et al., 2003, and Walker, 2003. All efforts were made to ensure this data was accurate; however, the reader should be aware that population numbers and status information are constantly being revised.

Gray Wolf *(Canis lupus)*
Physical Characteristics
Adult males can weigh from 45 to 175 pounds and have a total length (including the tail) of between 4 and 6 feet. Adult females are usually smaller and shorter in length than males. Northern wolves are generally heavier and larger than southern wolves. Gray wolves vary in coat color from pure white to coal black. The most common coloration is pale tan or cream mixed with black, brown and white. They can live 8 to 16 years in the wild, up to 20 in captivity.

Range Historically the gray wolf was found north of latitude 15°–20°N, including throughout nearly all of Eurasia and North America.

Current range
United States: Alaska, northern Minnesota, northern Wisconsin, Michigan's Upper Peninsula, parts of Montana, Washington, Idaho; reintroduced to Yellowstone National Park, 1995–96.

Canada: still occupies about 80 percent of its historic range; extirpated from Nova Scotia, New Brunswick, the island of Newfoundland; scarce or not found in highly developed or densely populated areas of other provinces and territories.
Eurasia: a few thousand wolves are scattered across isolated areas of Europe with populations holding steady or expanding in most areas; found in large forested areas of Eastern Europe, and in mountain and semi-desert areas of the Middle East; in wilderness areas of Russia and China.

Population and Status Varies throughout original range from extinct to relatively intact. The three main strongholds for the species are Alaska (approximately 6,000 wolves), Canada (40,000 to 60,000) and Russia (40,000 to 60,000). Only the subpopulations listed below are officially considered threatened.

Italian subpopulation *(Canis lupus)*
Population and Status Approximately 500 wolves. Vulnerable. Threatened by habitat loss, fragmentation and degradation; hybridization with dogs; poaching.

Mexican subpopulation *(Canis lupus baileyi). Also known as the Mexican wolf.*
Physical Characteristics
Smallest North American gray wolf.

Range Southernmost subspecies of gray wolf in North America. Once found in mountainous regions of Mexico and the southwestern United States.

Population and Status Officially extinct in the wild, largely due to predator-control measures. Exterminated from U.S. portion of range by the 1970s. No confirmed wild sightings in Mexico since 1980. Reintroductions began in Arizona and New Mexico in 1998. There are approximately 260 Mexican gray wolves in captivity. Despite the 2003 deaths of several animals from gunshots and vehicle accidents, about 30 to 40 wild wolves now live in Arizona and New Mexico.

Spanish-Portuguese subpopulation *(Canis lupus)*
Population and Status Approximately 1500 to 2500 wolves. Threatened by habit loss, fragmentation and degradation; hybridization with dogs; poaching.

Red Wolf *(Canis rufus)*
Physical Characteristics
Resembles gray wolf but is smaller: average-sized males weigh between 45 and 55 pounds and are about 4 to 5 feet long. Coloring resembles that of the average gray wolf but the red wolf's flanks and legs may have a reddish tinge. Lifespan is similar to that of the gray wolf.

Range Historically roamed forests and coastal plains from central Texas to southern Florida, possibly as far north as New England. Reintroduced into northeastern North Carolina.

Population and Status In 1980, the United States Fish and Wildlife Service rounded up the last free-ranging red wolves in the world and the species was declared extinct in the wild. Only 14 of the remaining animals were genetically pure enough to be used as the base of a captive breeding program. In 1987, four wolf pairs were reintroduced to North Carolina. Today more than 150 wolves form a captive breeding population and there are over 100 red wolves in the wild.

However, the species remains highly endangered, and the success of the reintroduction is threatened by the possibility of the wolves interbreeding with coyotes.

Recent DNA research indicates that red wolves are a distinct species but that there has been interbreeding with coyotes in the past. There is also a close genetic link between the "gray wolves" of the Great Lakes region of the U.S. and eastern Canada and red wolves. Many scientists believe the southeastern Canada population probably contains pure gray wolves and pure red wolves, as well as red wolf/coyote hybrids and red wolf/gray wolf hybrids. Sorting out the relationships is of more than scientific interest, because the existence of a wild red wolf population would affect the U.S. red wolf recovery program, which has an annual budget of approximately $4 million.

Ethiopian Wolf *(Canis simensis)* *Also known as Abyssinian wolf or Simien jackal.*
Physical Characteristics
Average-sized males weigh from 25 to 45 pounds and are about 45 to 55 inches long from nose to tail tip. Females are about 20 percent smaller than males. Ethiopian wolves have a short, soft, tawny red coat with pale ginger underfur. The inside parts of the ears, chest and underparts are white, as is a well defined band on the underside of the neck. Lifespan is unknown.

Range Confined to small, isolated areas of grassland in Ethiopia. The Bale Mountains are the home of the most important population group, which contains approximately 60 percent of the world's remaining Ethiopian wolves.

Population and Status The global population, estimated in 2003 to be about 500 animals, was gravely threatened by a rabies epidemic in 2003–04. A core population in the Web Valley of the Bale Mountains was nearly wiped out: out of an estimated pre-rabies population of 80 wolves, only 15 to 20 adult and subadult wolves remain. An emergency vaccination campaign appears to have been effective in confining the outbreak to the Web Valley; however, the species remains critically endangered. Threats include habitat loss and fragmentation; aggression from and hybridization with domestic dogs; disease.

Golden Jackal *(Canis aureus)*
Physical Characteristics
Adults weigh about 15 to 35 pounds and have a length, excluding the tail, of about 30 to 50 inches. Coat varies with the season and wolf's location but is usually yellowish to silvery gray. Lifespan is about 4 to 8 years, up to 16 in captivity.

Range From northern and eastern Africa across to the Middle East, southeastern Europe, and into southern Asia.

Population and Status Locally abundant and widespread. Adaptable in diet and able to do well near human settlements.

African Wild Dog *(Lycaon pictus)*
Physical Characteristics
Adults weigh about 45 to 70 pounds and have a body length of 30 to 45 inches. A white-tipped tail adds another 12 to 18 inches. Irregular white and yellow blotches break up the darkness of the short coat. The muzzle is dark. Lifespan is about 10 years.

Range Scattered, isolated pockets of Africa, from the Sahara to South Africa.

Population and Status Estimated to be fewer than 5,500. Endangered. Threatened by human persecution, road accidents, habitat loss, disease and predation by lions.

Dhole *(Cuon alpinus)* *Also known as Asian wild dog or red dog.*
Physical Characteristics
Adults weigh an average of 37 pounds and measure about 50 inches from nose to tail tip. They stand about 20 inches high at the shoulder. Coat is a sandy rust on top, paler underneath. Tail is black and bushy. May live 8 to 12 years in the wild, up to 16 in captivity.

Range Western Asia to China, India, Indochina to Java. Rare outside protected areas.

Population and Status Two of 10 subspecies — the East Asian dhole (*C. a. alpinus*) and the smaller West Asian dhole (*C. a. hesperius*) — are threatened. Two Indian subspecies — (*C. a. primaevus*) and (*C. a. laniger*) are rare. The two main threats to dholes throughout their range are habitat destruction and removal of their prey species. The creation of national parks and tiger reserves in India is helping to conserve dholes.

NOTES

See Bibliography for full reference information.

p. 18   "Blackfoot Creation myth" retold from Taylor, 1994. p. 24.

p. 21   Henry Beston, *The Outermost House*, New York. Ballantine Books, 1971. p. 67.

p. 25   "about 300,000 years ago" Wilson et al., 2000.

p. 26   "Cree legend" Mercatante, 1999. p. 73.

p. 32   "Pawnee myth" retold from Dorsey, 1904. pp. 14–20 and in Lopez, 1995. p. 34

p. 39   "Dzawada'enuxw (Kwakiutl) myth" Williams, 2001. p. 9.

p. 51   "mile and a half downwind" Mech, 1970. p. 197.

p. 51   Seaton, 1937. p. 1.

p. 52   "covered over 500 miles" Paquet et al., 2003, under "Dispersal."

p. 54   Theberge, 1971. p. 42.

p. 58   "Turkish legend" retold from Basilov, 1989. p. 55.

p. 58   "Déné myth" retold from Reynolds and Garr, 1973. pp. 14–18.

p. 59   "Greek legend" retold from several sources including Newton, 2002. pp. 3–5.

p. 60   "suckled by a wolf" Newton, 2002. p. 5.

p. 61   "changes your life" Black, 1999. p. 53.

p. 64   "Tsistsistas legend" Schlesier, 1987. pp. 77–78, 82.

p. 76   "punishes that foot by biting it" Barber, 1993. p. 70.

p. 76   Oppian, 1928. pp. 139–141.

p. 79   "large pieces of meat" Mech, 1970. p. 169.

p. 80   "May 1 and October 1" Paquet et al., 2003. under "Kill and Consumption Rates."

p. 84   "state of Uttar Pradesh, India" Ehrenreich, 1997. p. 44.

p. 95   "from Hrafnsmál, tenth-century Norse poem" Davidson, 1978. p. 133.

p. 95   "soak through every sinew" from *Gesta Danorum* (Story of the Danes).

p. 96   Sturluson, 1923. p. 210.

p. 98   "Song of a Tsistsistas (Cheyenne) scout" Schlesier, 1987. p. 3.

p. 101   "the Cheyenne would be able to kill" Powell, 1979. pp. 16–17.

p. 103   "gang of wolves" Skinner, 1975. pp. 686–87.

p. 103   "Gray Hawk's song" Densmore, 1918. p. 339.

p. 109   Karok Shaman's Song quoted in Soens, 1999. p. 117.

p. 114   Boas story cited in Campbell, 1983. pp. 190–191.

p. 114   Hunt, 2002. p. 52.

p. 115   "it doesn't hurt him" Kluckhohn, 1944. p. 203.

p. 127   Young, 1946, preface (n.p.).

p. 128   "great respect for the wolf" Boitani, 1995. p. 8.

p. 131   "beautiful and wholesome deeds" Barber, 1993. pp. 70–71.

p. 131   "wolf did to the lambkin" Flores, 1996. p. 55.

p. 133   "animals which are not wild" Turville-Petre, 1964. p. 61.

p. 137   " souls like we have" Rasmussen, 1976. p. 56.

p. 138   "expect to be treated better" Pollard, 1964. p. 149.

p. 138   "spiritual fortitude of the community" Boitani, 1995. p. 5.

p. 143   "increased game numbers" Grooms, 2003. p. 12.

p. 150   "Blessing offered by Nez Perce elder" Hampton, 1997. p. 225.

p. 154   "80 percent of their historic range" Paquet, 2003. pp. 42–43.

p. 154   "Montana, Idaho and Wyoming" United States Fish and Wildlife Service, 2003.

p. 154   "living in the wild today" United States Fish and Wildlife Service, 2003.

p. 156   "probably ten or fewer" Boitani, 2000. Table 1.

p. 156   "killed 26 wolves from 2000 to 2002" State of the Environment in Norway, 2003.

p. 158   "poachers claim about 20 percent of the population" Yakutchik, 2003.

p. 162   "before wolves returned to Yellowstone" Jones, 2002.

p. 162   "in Montana and Wyoming" Johnson, 2003.

p. 162   "says Yellowstone Wolf Project Leader Doug Smith" Johnson, 2003.

PHOTO CREDITS

All photographs are by Daniel J. Cox unless otherwise indicated.

p. 4   Kit Weiss, The National Museum of Denmark

p. 14   Postcard from the collection of Peter Schleifenbaum

p. 15   © Canadian Museum of Civilization, catalogue no. VII-B-15 a-c, photo Harry Foster, image no. S92-4166

p. 28   From the design by Sir E. Burne-Jones

p. 29   Ohio Historical Society

p. 31   © Canadian Museum of Civilization, catalogue no. VII-B-5, photo Harry Foster, image no. S85-3271

p. 33   Pekka Parviainen/Science Photo Library

p. 40   Royal British Columbia Museum, catalogue number 15747

p. 52   Courtesy of the Burke Museum of Natural History and Culture, catalogue number 25.0/47, Tlingit Crest Hat, collected at Fort Wrangell

p. 57   Photograph by Bob Hanson. AMNH 2381 (16/2359)

p. 60   Glenbow Archives ND-1-180

p. 61   *top* Werner Forman Archives *bottom* © Canadian Museum of Civilization, catalogue no. VII-C-1800, photo Harry Foster

p. 75   Werner Forman Archives

p. 81   *top and bottom* John James Audubon

p. 94   Werner Forman Archives

p. 98   Edward S. Curtis Collection, Library of Congress 3B44614U

p. 99   Thaw Collection, Fenimore Art Museum, Cooperstown, New York. Photograph by John Bigelow Taylor, NYC

p. 102   © CORBIS

p. 104   Glenbow Archives NA-667-6

p. 105   Purse lid, from the Sutton Hoo Ship Burial, c.625–30 AD (gold, garnets and millefiori glass), Anglo-Saxon School, (7th century) / British Museum, London, UK, Boltin Picture Library; / Bridgeman Art Library

p. 112   Werner Forman Archives

p. 116   By permission of the British Library

p. 118   Royal British Columbia Museum, catalogue number 13863

p. 119   She-Wolf, c.500 BC with figures of Romulus and Remus by Antonio Pollaiuolo (1433–98) c.1484–96 (bronze), Etruscan (6th century BC) / Museo Capitolino, Rome, Italy / Bridgeman Art Library

p. 131   By permission of the British Library

p. 133   © Underwood & Underwood/CORBIS

p. 134   Postcard from the collection of Peter Schleifenbaum

p. 135   American Museum of Natural History A/649

p. 137   © Canadian Museum of Civilization, catalogue no. VII-A-320 a-b, photo Harry Foster

p. 142   Royal British Columbia Museum, catalogue number 16504

p. 147   Royal British Columbia Museum, catalogue number 16343

p. 165   From the collection of Peter Schleifenbaum

p. 168   *top right* Robert Winslow/maXximages.com *bottom right* James Robinson/maXximages.com

p. 169   *top left* BPL/M/ Harvey/maXximages.com *top right* ABPL/maXximages.com *bottom left* Francois Savigny/maXximages.com *bottom right* Ralph Reinhold/maXximages.com

back cover   *top right* © Canadian Museum of Civilization, catalogue no. VII-C-1800, photo Harry Foster *bottom right* By permission of the British Library

Images on pages 21, 26, 32, 39, 58, 59, 69, 87, 93, 96,101, 111, 114, 125, 128, 130, 136, 153 © 2005 JupiterImages Corporation

BIBLIOGRAPHY

These books served as valuable reference works for this volume.

Bomford, Liz. *The Complete Wolf.* New York: St. Martins Press, 1993.

Busch, Robert H. *The Wolf Almanac.* Markham, ON: Fitzhenry & Whiteside, 1995.

Lopez, Barry Holstun. *Of Wolves and Men.* New York: Touchstone, 1995.

Mech, L. David and Luigi Boitani (eds.). *Wolves: Behavior, Ecology, and Conservation.* Chicago: University of Chicago Press, 2003.

Rehnmark, Eva-Lena. *Neither God Nor Devil: Rethinking Our Perception of Wolves.* San Francisco: Pomegranate, 2000.

The following sources offer the interested reader a chance to continue exploring the world of wolves. Space restrictions do not allow a complete listing of resources.

Aelian. *On the Characteristics of Animals.* English translation by A.F. Scholfield. The Loeb Classical Library. Cambridge, MA: Harvard University Press, 1958–59.

Arima, Eugene and John Dewhirst. "Nootkans of Vancouver Island," in *Handbook of North American Indians,* vol. 7, Northwest Coast. Washington, DC: Smithsonian Institution Press, 1990.

Bangs, Ed and John Shivik. "Managing Wolf Conflict with Livestock in the Northwestern United States." *Carnivore Damage Prevention News* 3: 2–5, July 2001.

Barber, Richard (trans.). *Bestiary: Being an English Version of the Bodleian Library, Oxford m.s. Bodley 764 with All the Original Miniatures Reproduced in Facsimile.* Woodbridge, Suffolk, UK: Boydell Press, 1993.

Baring-Gould, Sabine. *The Book of Were-Wolves.* London: 1865; New York: Causeway Books, 1973 (reprint).

Basilov, Vladimir N. (ed.). *Nomads of Eurasia.* Seattle: University of Washington Press, 1989.

Black, Martha. *HuupuKwanum Tupaat: Out of the Mist: Treasures of the Nuu-chah-nulth Chiefs.* Victoria: Royal British Columbia Museum, 1999.

Boas, Franz. *The Social Organization and the Secret Societies of the Kwakiutl Indians.* Report of the U.S. National Museum. Washington, DC: 1895; New York: Johnson Reprint Corporation, 1970 (reprint).

Boitani, Luigi. "Ecological and Cultural Diversities in the Evolution of Wolf-Human Relationships," in *Ecology and Conservation of Wolves in a Changing World,* L.N. Carbyn, S. H. Fritts and D.R. Seip (eds.). Edmonton, AB: Canadian Circumpolar Institute, 1995.

————. *Action Plan for the Conservation of the Wolves* (Canis lupus) *in Europe.* Convention on the Conservation of European Wildlife and Natural Habitats (Bern Convention), *Nature and Environment, No. 113.* Council of Europe Publishing, 2000.

Campbell, Joseph. *Historical Atlas of World Mythology,* vol. 1, *The Way of the Animal Powers.* London: Times Books Limited, 1983.

Chamberlain, Von Del. *When Stars Came Down to Earth: Cosmology of the Skidi Pawnee Indians of North America.* Los Altos, CA: Ballena Press, 1982.

Chase, Richard, Jr. and David Teasley. "Little Red Riding Hood: Werewolf and Prostitute." *The Historian* 57(4): 769–76. Summer 1995.

Clarke, C.H.D. "The Beast of Gévaudan." *Natural History* 80(4): 44–51, 66–73. April 1971.

Cronyn, George W. (ed.). *American Indian Poetry: An Anthology of Songs and Chants.* New York: Fawcett Columbine, 1918, 1991.

Curtis, Edward S. *The North American Indian,* 20 volumes. Self-published 1907–30. Reprinted by New York: Johnson Reprint Corporation, 1970.

Davidson, H.R. Ellis. "Shape-changing in the Old Norse Sagas," in *Animals in Folklore.* J.R. Porter and W.M.S. Russell, (eds.). Cambridge, UK: D.S. Brewer Ltd., 1978.

————. *Myths and Symbols in Pagan Europe.* Syracuse, NY: Syracuse University Press, 1988.

Densmore, Frances. Teton Sioux Music. *Bureau of American Ethnology Bulletin,* no. 61. Washington, DC: Government Printing Office, 1918.

Dorsey, George A. *Traditions of the Skidi Pawnee.* Memoirs of the American Folklore Society, vol. 8. Boston: Houghton, Mifflin and Co. for the American Folklore Society, 1904; New York: Kraus Reprint Co., 1969 (reprint).

Eckels, Richard Preston. *Greek Wolf-lore.* Ph.D. diss. Philadelphia, PA: University of Pennsylvania, 1937.

Ehrenreich, Barbara. *Blood Rites: Origins and History of the Passions of War.* Markham, ON: Fitzhenry & Whiteside, 1997.

Eisler, Robert. *Man into Wolf: An Anthropological Interpretation of Sadism, Masochism, and Lycanthropy.* London: Spring Books, n.d.[c.1951].

Erdoes, Richard and Alfonso Ortiz (eds.). *American Indian Myths and Legends.* New York: Pantheon Books, 1984.

Ernst, Alice Henson. *The Wolf Ritual of the Northwest Coast.* Eugene, OR: University of Oregon Press, 1952.

Fascione, Nina, Lisa G.L. Osborn, Stephen R. Kendrot, and Paul C. Paquet. "Canis soupus: Eastern Wolf Genetics and Its Implications for Wolf Recovery in the Northeast United States." *Endangered Species Update,* 18(4): 159–64. July–August 2001.

Fiennes, Richard. *The Order of Wolves.* Indianapolis, IN: Bobbs-Merrill, 1976.

Flores, Nona C. (ed.). *Animals in the Middle Ages.* New York: Garland Publishing, Inc., 1996.

Fuller, T.K. and L.B. Keith. "Wolf Population Dynamics and Prey Relationships in Northeastern Alberta." *Journal of Wildlife Management,* 44: 583–602. 1980.

Gershenson, Daniel E. Apollo the Wolf-god. *Journal of Indo-European Studies*, monograph no. 8. McLean, VA: Institute for the Study of Man, 1991.

Grinnell, George Bird. *Pawnee Hero Stories and Folk-tales*. New York: Forest and Stream Publishing Company, 1889; Lincoln: University of Nebraska Press, 1961 (reprint).

Grooms, Steve. "Wolf Control Controversies." *International Wolf*, 11–13. Fall 2003.

Hall, Robert L. *An Archaeology of the Soul: North American Indian Belief and Ritual*. Urbana and Chicago: University of Illinois Press, 1997.

Hampton, Bruce. *The Great American Wolf*. New York: Henry Holt & Company, 1997.

Hassrick, Royal B. *The Sioux: Life and Customs of a Warrior Society*. Norman: University of Oklahoma Press, 1964.

Hunt, Norman Bancroft. *Shamanism in North America*. Toronto: Key Porter Books, 2002.

Irimoto, Takashi and Takako Yamada (eds.). *Circumpolar Religion and Ecology: An Anthropology of the North*. Tokyo: University of Tokyo Press, 1994.

Jenness, Diamond. *The Life of the Copper Eskimos*. Report of the Canadian Arctic Expedition 1913–1918, vol. 12. Ottawa, ON: F. A. Acland, 1922.

Johnson, Shelli. Wolves in Yellowstone Are Most Visible in the World. YellowstonePark.com. www.yellowstonepark.com/news/details.asp?newsid=6. 2003.

————. Yellowstone Park's Wolf Population Grows from 132 to 148 Animals; 37-member Druid Peak Pack Breaks into Four Packs in 2002. YellowstonePark.com. www.yellowstonepark.com/features/Druid051305.shtml. 2003.

Jones, Karen. "Fighting Outlaws, Returning Wolves." *History Today* 52(3): 38–40. March 2002.

Kluckhohn, Clyde. *Navaho Witchcraft*. Boston, MA: Beacon Press, 1944.

Knight, John. "On the Extinction of the Japanese Wolf." *Asian Folklore Studies* 56:1, 129–59. April, 1997.

Kroeber, A.L. "Indian Myths of South Central California." *Publications in American Archaeology and Ethnology*, vol. 4, no. 4. Berkeley: University of California Press, 1907.

Lange, Karen E. "Wolf to Woof: The Evolution of Dogs." *National Geographic* 201(2): 2–11. January 2002.

Leonard, J. A., R.K. Wayne, J. Wheeler, R., et al. "Ancient DNA Evidence for Old World Origin of New World Dogs." *Science* 298 (5598): 1613–16. November 22, 2002.

Lowie, Robert H. *The Religion of the Crow Indians*. Anthropological Papers of the American Museum of Natural History, vol. 25, part 2. New York: American Museum of Natural History, 1922.

Maclean, Charles and Allen Lane. *The Wolf Children*. London: Penguin Books, 1977.

Mails, Thomas E. *The Mystic Warriors of the Plains*. Garden City, NY: Doubleday & Company, 1972.

————. *Dog Soldier Societies of the Plains*. New York: Marlowe & Company. 1973, 1998

Marino, J. "Threatened Ethiopian Wolves Persist in Small Isolated African Enclaves." *Oryx* 37:62–71, 2003.

McIlwraith, T. F. *The Bella Coola Indians*, vol. 1. Toronto: University of Toronto Press, 1948.

McIntyre, Rick (ed.). *War Against the Wolf: America's Campaign to Exterminate the Wolf*. Stillwater, MN: Voyageur Press, 1995.

McMillion, Scott. "Yellowstone Reports Wolf Sightings Every Day for Almost Three Years." *Bozeman Daily Chronicle*, December 14, 2003.

Mech, L. David. *The Wolf: The Ecology and Behavior of an Endangered Species*. Minneapolis: University of Minnesota Press, 1970.

Mech, L. David, Layne G. Adams, Thomas J. Meier, John W. Burch and Bruce W. Dale. *The Wolves of Denali*. Minneapolis: University of Minnesota Press, 1998.

Menon, Shanti. Man's Oldest Friend. *Discover* 18(1): 86, January 1998.

Mercatante, Anthony S. *Zoo of the Gods*. Berkeley, CA: Seastone. 1999.

Mooney, James. *Myths of the Cherokee and Sacred Formulas of the Cherokees*. 19th and 7th Bureau of American Ethnology Annual Reports. Nashville, TN: Charles and Randy Elder, 1982 (reprint).

Morgan, W. *Human Wolves Among the Navaho*. Yale University Publications in Anthropology, No. 11. New Haven, CT: Yale University Press, 1936.

Murie, James R. *Pawnee Indian Societies*. Anthropological Papers of the American Museum of Natural History, Vol. 11, Part 7. New York: American Museum of Natural History, 1914.

Newton, Michael. *Savage Girls and Wild Boys*. London: Faber and Faber, 2002.

Nowak, Ronald M. "The Original Status of Wolves in Eastern North America." *Southeastern Naturalist* 1(2): 95–130. 2002.

Ogier, Darryl. "Night Revels and Werewolfery in Calvinist Guernsey." *Folklore Annual* 109: 53–62. Folklore Society, 1998.

Oppian. *Oppian, Colluthus, Tryphiodorus*. English translation by A.W. Mair, London: Heinemann, 1928.

Otten, Charlotte F. (ed.). *A Lycanthropy Reader: Werewolves in Western Culture*. Syracuse, NY: Syracuse University Press, 1986.

Paquet, P. C. and L. N. Carbyn. "Wolf, *Canis lupus*, and Allies." In *Wild Mammals of North America: Biology, Management, and Conservation*. G.A. Feldhamer, B.C. Thompson, and J.A. Chapman (eds.). Baltimore, MD: Johns Hopkins University Press, 2003.

Person, David K., R. Terry Bowyer and Victor Van Ballenberghe. "Density Dependence of Ungulates and Functional Responses of Wolves: Effects on Predator-Prey Ratios." *Alces* 37(2): 253–73, Spring 2001.

Peters, Roger. *Dance of the Wolves*. New York: McGraw-Hill, 1985.

Peterson, Rolf O. *The Wolves of Isle Royale: A Broken Balance*. Minocqua, WI: Willow Creek Press, 1995.

Pollard, John. *Wolves and Werewolves*. London: Robert Hale, 1964.

Powell, James V. "Quileute," in *Handbook of North American Indians*, vol. 7, Northwest Coast. Washington, DC: Smithsonian Institution Press, 1990.

Powell, Peter J. *People of the Sacred Mountain*. New York: Harper & Row, 1979.

Rabon, David R., Jr. "From Fourteen: A Beginning." *International Wolf* 14(1): 10–11, Spring 2004.

Rasmussen, Knud. "Intellectual Culture of the Iglulik Eskimos." Report of the Fifth Thule Expedition 1921–24, vol. 7, no. 1. Copenhagen: Gyldendal, 1929; New York: AMS Press Inc., 1976 (reprint).

Reynolds, Margaret and Benn Garr. *Legends of Déné*. Saskatoon: Saskatchewan Indian Cultural College, Curriculum Development Unit, 1973.

Sablin, M.V. and G.A. Khlopachev. "The Earliest Ice Age Dogs: Evidence from Eliseevichi 1." *Current Anthropology* 43(5): 795–99. 2002.

Savolainen, P., Y.P. Zhang, J. Luo, J. Lundeberg, and T. Leitner. "Genetic Evidence for an East Asian Origin of Domestic Dogs." *Science* 298 (5598): 1610–13. November 22, 2002.

Sax, Boria. *Animals in the Third Reich: Pets, Scapegoats, and the Holocaust.* New York: Continuum International Publishing Group Inc., 2000.

Schleidt, Wolfgang M., and Michael D. Shalter. "Co-evolution of Humans and Canids: An Alternative View of Dog Domestication: *Homo Homini Lupus?*" *Evolution and Cognition* 9(1): 57–72, 2003.

Schlesier, Karl H. *The Wolves of Heaven: Cheyenne Shamanism, Ceremonies, and Prehistoric Origins*. Norman: University of Oklahoma Press, 1987.

Seton, Ernest Thompson. *Great Historic Animals: Mainly About Wolves*. New York: Charles Scribner's Sons, 1937.

Sharpe, Virginia A, Bryan G. Norton and Strachan Donnelley. *Wolves and Human Communities: Biology, Politics, and Ethics*. Washington, DC: Island Press, 2001.

Skinner, Alanson. "Societies of the Iowa," in *Societies of the Plains Indians*, Clark Wissler (ed.). Anthropological Papers of the American Museum of Natural History, vol. 11, published in 13 parts. New York: American Museum of Natural History, 1912–1916; New York: AMS Press, Inc., 1975 (reprint).

Soens, A. L. *I, The Song: Classical Poetry of Native North America*. Salt Lake: University of Utah Press, 1999.

State of Environment in Norway: Large Predators. www.environment. no/templates/PrintThemeParge. aspx?id+2251.2003

Stauth, David. Wolves Are Rebalancing Yellowstone Ecosystem. www. eurekalert.org/pub_releases/2003-10/ osu-war102803.php. October 28, 2003.

Steinhart, Peter. *The Company of Wolves*. New York: Alfred A. Knopf, 1995.

Sturluson, Snorri. *The Prose Edda*. Brodeur, Arthur Gilchrist, (trans.). New York: The American-Scandinavian Foundation, 1923.

Swanton, John R. *Myths and Tales of the Southeastern Indians*. Bureau of American Ethnology Bulletin 88. Washington, DC: Government Printing Office, 1929.

Taylor, Colin F. ed. consultant. *Native American Myths and Legends*. Vancouver, BC: Cavendish Books, 1994.

Theberge, John B. "Wolf Music." *Natural History* 80(4): 37–32. April 1971.

_____. *Wolves and Wilderness*. Toronto: Dent Canada, 1975.

Thompson, Stith. *Tales of the North American Indians*. Bloomington: Indiana University Press, 1929.

Turi, Johan. *Turi's Book of Lappland*. (E.G. Nash, trans.). Anthropological Publications. Oosterhout, The Netherlands: 1931, 1966.

Turville-Petre, E.O.G. *Myth and Religion of the North: The Religion of Ancient Scandinavia*. New York: Holt, Rinehart and Winston, 1964.

United States Fish and Wildlife Service. Gray Wolf Biologue Fact Sheet. midwest.fws. gov/wolf/learn/biologue.htm. 2003.

Vila, Carlos, Peter Savolainen, Jesus E. Maldonado, et al. "Multiple and Ancient Origins of the Domestic Dog." *Science* 276 (5319): 1687–89. June 13, 1997.

_____. "Red Wolves Back From Extinction in U.S. Wild." *National Geographic News*. January 31, 2003.

Walker, Dale L. *The Boys of '98, Theodore Roosevelt and the Rough Riders*. New York: Tom Doherty Associates, Inc., 1998.

Walker, J.R. *The Sun Dance and Other Ceremonies of the Oglala Division of the Teton Dakota*. Anthropological Papers of the American Museum of Natural History, vol. 16, part 2. New York: American Museum of Natural History, 1917.

Wayne, Robert K. "Molecular Evolution of the Dog Family." *Trends in Genetics* 9: 218–24. 1993.

Williams, Judith. *Two Wolves at the Dawn of Time: Kingcome Inlet Pictographs, 1893–1998*. Vancouver: New Star Books, 2001.

Wilmers, Christopher C., Daniel R., Stahler, Robert L. Crabtree, et al. "Resource Dispersion and Consumer Dominance: Scavenging at Wolf- and Hunter-killed Carcasses in Greater Yellowstone, USA." *Ecology Letters* 6(11): 996–1003. 2003.

Wilson, P.J., S. Grewal, I.D. Lawford, J.N.M. Heal, et al. "DNA Profiles of the Eastern Canadian Wolf and the Red Wolf Provide Evidence for a Common Evolutionary History Independent of the Gray Wolf." *Canadian Journal of Zoology* 78: 2156–66. 2000.

Wissler, Clark. *Social Organization and Ritualistic Ceremonies of the Blackfoot Indians*. Anthropological Papers of the American Museum of Natural History, vol. 7. New York: American Museum of Natural History, 1912; New York: AMS Press, Inc., 1975 (reprint).

_____. "General Discussion of Shamanistic and Dancing Societies," in *Societies of the Plains Indians*, Clark Wissler (ed.). Anthropological Papers of the American Museum of Natural History, vol. 11, published in 13 parts. New York: American Museum of Natural History, 1912–1916, New York. AMS Press, Inc., 1975 (reprint).

_____. "Societies and Ceremonial Associations in the Oglala Division of the Teton-Dakota," in *Societies of the Plains Indians*, Clark Wissler (ed.). Anthropological Papers of the American Museum of Natural History, vol. 11, published in 13 parts. New York: American Museum of Natural History, 1912–1916; New York: AMS Press, Inc., 1975 (reprint).

Wolves in American Culture Committee. *Wolf: A Modern Look*. Ashland, WI: NorthWord Inc., 1986.

Yakutchik, Maryalice. Ciao, Il Lupo! *Discovery Communications* animal.discovery. com/convbergence/wolves/dispatches/ dispatch1.html. 2003.

Young, Stanley. *The Wolf in North American History*. Caldwell, ID: The Caxton Printers, 1946.

Zipes, Jack. *The Trials and Tribulations of Little Red Riding Hood*. South Hadley, MA: Bergin & Garvey Publishers, Inc., 1984.

INDEX

References to images and captions are indicated by *italicized* page numbers.

Absaroke people, *98*
Abyssinian wolves. *See* Ethiopian wolves
Aesop's fables, 125, 129
African wild dogs (*Lycaon pictus*), 22, 169
Ahtna people, 135
Ainu people, 76
Alaska, 27, 144, 146
Alberta, 56, 80
Alexander, Hartley, 90
Algonquin Park, Canada, 84
Alpha Canis Majoris (Sirius), 21, 29, *33*
alpha wolves, 40, 42, *51*
Amala, 56
American Horse, 104
Amos, Patrick, *40*
ancient Chinese, 21, 29, 30
ancient Greeks, 28
Andrus, Herbert, 52
Apollo Lykeios, 28
Arctic tundra, 42
Arikara people, 27, 137
Arms of Viscount Wolseley, 101
Asia, 144
Asian wild dog. *See* dhole
attacks on humans, 82, 84, 87
Aua, 137
Audubon, John James, *80*
Axtell, Horace, 150
Aztec medicine, 116

Baden-Powell, Robert, 59
Bailey Wildlife Foundation Proactive Carnivore Conservation Fund, 143
baleen wolf-killers, 135
Banff National Park, Alberta, 56
bears, 95
Beast of Gévaudan, 84
Bella Bella carving, *147*
Bella Coola (Nuxalk) people, 57, 113, 114, 116, 118
Beowulf, 94
berserkrs, 95
bestiaries, 131
Beston, Henry, 21

Bieszczady National Park, 155
"big bad wolf," 13
Bird Shirt, 112
birth of pups, 45
black American wolf, *81*
Blackfoot people, 18, 29, *69*, 102, *104*
body language, 49, 51
body parts, *116*, 118
Boitani, Luigi, 128, 138
Bowstrings, 101
brain, 143
breeding, 42
British Columbia, 84, 143
brooch, *142*
Brothers Grimm, 129
bure uy, 112

Caddo people, 27
Calcutta, India, 39, 56
Calusa people, 75
Canada, 80, 84, 136, 143, 144, 146, 154. *See also names of individual locations*
Canidae family, 21
Canis, 21, 22, 26, 72, 168–69
Canis aureus (golden jackals), 22, 169
Canis dirus (dire wolves), 25, 26
Canis familiaris (domestic dogs), 22, 56, 128
Canis latrans (coyotes), 22, 25
Canis lupus (gray wolves), 13, 168
Canis lupus baileyi (Mexican wolves), 168
Canis rufus (red wolves), 22, 25, 168–69
Canis simensis (Ethiopian wolves), 22, 169
Canute the Great, 130
captive wolves, 161
care of cubs, 39, 45–46, 49
care of human children, 39, 56–57, 59, 60
Caribou Inuit people, 128
Carmathen, Wales, 84
Carpathian mountains, 22
carvings, *147*
Catlin, George, 102
Celestial Wolf, 29. *See also* Sirius
ceremonies and rituals, 60–61, 93–119, 136

Native North American, 60–61, 98–105, 112–16, 119
shamans, 101–102, 112–16, 119
Viking, 94–95
wolf societies, 60–61, 104–105
Chaney, Jr., Lon, *133*
Charlemagne, 138
Chemehuevi legends, 27
Cherokee people, 134
Cheyenne people, 93, 101, 105, 137
Chilcotin shamans, 113
China, 146
Chinese legends, 21, 29, 30
Chipewyan legends, 58
coat, 168, 169
Co-evolution of Humans and Canids, 84
Colorado, 161
Comanche people, 135
communication, 49, 51
Company of Wolves, The, *153*, *159*
compensation programs, 140, 142, 143
control programs, 143, 144, 155, 159
Copper Eskimos (Copper Inuit), 115
copulatory tie, 42
Coyote (legendary character), 27
coyotes (*Canis latrans*), 22, 25
Crazy Horse, 93, 104
Cree people, 26
Crisler, Lois, *159*
Croatia, 140
Crow people, 28–29, 98
Cub Scouts, 59
cubs, 38, 40, 45–46, *47*, 49
Cuon alpinus (dhole), 22, 169
Cynegetica, 76
Cynodictis, 22
daggers, *99*
Dakota people, 45, 58
Dance of the Wolves, 125
Dark Ages, 130
deadfalls, 135, 137
Defenders of Wildlife, 140, 143
dens, 42, 44, 45, 46, 49
Déné people, 58
Denmark, 138
Densmore, Frances, 103
dhole (*Cuon alpinus*), 22, 169
diet, 69, 77, 79
dire wolves (*Canis dirus*), 25, 26

distances traveled, 145
DNA studies, 25, 56
dog star (Sirius), 21, 29, *33*
dogs (*Canis familiaris*), 22, 56, 128
domestication, 56, 128
dominance, 39, 40, 51
dung, 52, 116
Dzawada'enuxw, 39

ecological flexibility, 39
ecosystems, 80, 82
Edda, The, 96
Edward the Confessor, 130
Endangered Species Act (ESA), 161, 164
England, *105*, 138
Environmental Impact Statement, 162
Ernst, Alice Henson, 60
ESA (Endangered Species Act), 161, 164
Eskimo wolf mask, 27
Ethiopian wolves (*Canis simensis*), 22, 169
Europe, 138, 144, 155, 158, 159. *See also names of individual locations*
eyes, 46

feces, 52, 116
feeding, 79
females, 40, 42–46, 49
Fenrir, *28*, 96
feral children, 39, 56–57, 59–60, 118
Fiennes, Richard, 143
Finland, 156
food. *See* diet
"Fool," 114
"Fools-the-Wolf," 29
fossils, *22*
Fox, Michael W., *158*
France, 84, 101, *133*, 138, 142
Freki, *28*
Freuchen, Peter, 114
fur trade, 126, 144, 146

game management, 143, 144
Garland, Hamlin, 136
Garnier, Gilles, *133*, 134
Genghis Khan, 58
genus Canis. *See* Canis

Geri, 28
German Wolf Child of Hesse, 56
Germany, 101, 155
Gévaudan, France, 84
Ghost Head, 105
Girgenti, Italy, 116
golden jackals (*Canis aureus*), 22, 169
Gray Hawk, 103
gray wolves (*Canis lupus*), 13, 168
Great Historic Animals, 51
Greater Yellowstone Ecosystem, 80, 153, 159, 162
Greek legends, 28

habitats, 26, 39, 154
Haida people, *15*, 112, *142*
Haliburton, Ontario, 87
Hati, 28
hats, *137*
Head Chief Big Belly, *104*
headdresses, *118*
heraldry, 101
Hidatsa people, 103, 112
hierarchies, 39, 40, 51, 75
Hillerman, Tony, 116
Hitchiti people, 26
Hitler, Adolf, 155
Hobbes, Thomas, 129
Hopi people, 80
howling, 52, 102
hrafnsmal, 95
humans,
    compared with wolves, 72, 75
    effect on wolf populations, 136
    feral children, 39, 56–57, 59–60, 118
    intimate relationships with wolves, 57–59
    killing of wolves, 125–47, 158, 159
    legends of. *See* legends
    wolf attacks on, 82, 84, 87
Hunt, Norman Bancroft, 114
hunting, 69–87
    attack, 77, 79
    by cubs, 49
    effect on ecosystem, 80, 82
    frequency of kills, 80
    packs and, 77, 79
    scent and, 77
    selection of prey, 69
    skills, 76
    styles, 72, 75
    of wolves by humans, 125–47, 158, 159
hybrids, 169
Ice Ages, 22, 25, 69, 71, 72, 128

Idaho, 140, 150
Iglulik Inuit people, 137
In Praise of Wolves, 93
India, 39, 56, 84
Inland Eskimo peoples, 136
intelligence, 143
Inuit legends, 26, 28, 58
Iowa people, 102
Ireland, 138
Isle Royale, Michigan, 82, 138
Israel, 56
Italy, *101*, 116, 136, 142, 158, 168

Japanese netsuke, *165*
jaw fossil, *22*
Julius Caesar, 118

Kaibab Southern Paiute people, 27
Kamala, 56
Kamchatka legends, 57
Karok shaman's song, 111
Kazan (Volga) Tatar shaman, 112
Keitlah, Nelson, 61
killing of wolves, 125–47, 158, 159
    control programs, 143, 144, 155, 159
    in Europe, 129–31, 138, 140, 158
    fur trade, 144, 146
    livestock protection, 142–44, 158
    in North America, 134–37, 138, 140
    poaching, 159
    for sport, 146
    timeline, 138
    werewolves, 130–34
King Edgar, 138
Kipling, Rudyard, 36, 59
Kluckhohn, Clyde, 115
Klukwalle ritual, 61, 104
Kostyack, John, 161
Krisuk, 114, 115
Kwakiutl (Kwakwaka'wakw) people, 57, 60, 61, 104, 112, 114, 137
Kyrgyzstan, 155

Lakota people, 27
Lapps (Saami), 128
Lawrence, R.D., 93
legends,
    ancient Chinese, 21, 29, 30
    of feral children, 56–57, 59–60, 118
    Greek, 28
    Native North American, 21, 26–32, 57, 58, 66

Norse, 28
    Turkish, 40, 58
    of wolf-human relationships, 57–59
leg-hold traps, 144
length,
    of *Canis* species, 168, 169
    of wolves (*Canis lupus*), 168
lifespan,
    of *Canis* species, 168, 169
    of wolves (*Canis lupus*), *133*, 168
litters, 42
Little Red Riding Hood, 13, *14*, 125, 129
liver, 116
livestock, 142–44, 156, 158, 160
lone wolves, 40, 41, 42, 52
Lopez, Barry, 75
Louveterie, 138
Lucky-Man, 27
Lupus, Sir Charles, 101
Lycaon pictus (African wild dog), 22, 169
Lyceum, 28

Magnus, Olaus, 133
Makah ritual, 60, 104
male wolves, 49
Man-Afraid of His Horses, 104
Mandan people, 137
Marie de France, 131
masks, *27, 57, 75*
Massachusetts, 138
mate preferences, *51*
mating, 42
Mech, L. David, 51, 79, 164
Medicinals from Animals, 116
medieval Europe, 129, 130
Mexican wolves (*Canis lupus baileyi*), 168
miacids, 22
Michigan, 82, 138, 154
Middle Ages, 94, 116, 130
Miletus, 59
Minnesota, 138, 140, 154, 164
mitochondrial DNA, 56
Montana, 138, 140, 154, 162
Mother Theresa, 56
"Mowgli's Brothers," 59
Muldoe, Earl, *119*
myths. *See* legends

National Wildlife Federation, 161
Native North Americans. *See also names of individual peoples*
    legends, 21, 26–32, 57, 58, 66

rituals, 60–61, 98–105, 112–16, 119
Navajo (Dineh) people, 115
Nazis, 155
Neither God Nor Devil, 82
netsuke, *165*
New York Times, 84
Newhouse, Sewell, 144
Nez Perce people, 142, 150, 164
Nietzsche, Friedrich, 155
Nisga'a art, *61*
Nootka (Nuu-chah-nulth) ritual, 60
Norsemen. *See* Vikings
North America, 134–37, 138, 140, 159. *See also names of individual locations*
Norway, 140, 156
Norwegian legends, 28
Nuu-chah-nulth (Nootka) art, 61

Ocean Woman, 27
Odin, 28, 94, 105
Of Wolves and Men, 75
Oglala people, 93, 98, 102, 104
Omaha people, 103, 160
Ontario, 84, 87
Order of Wolves, The, 143
Oregon, 161
origins of, 21
Outermost House, The, 21
Ovid, 59
Owl-Man, 101

packs, 39–62
    courtship in, 42
    defined, 40
    frequency of kills, 80
    hierarchies, 39, 40, 51, 75
    hunting in, 77, 79
    pups, 40, 46, 49
    scent-marking, 51–52
    size of, 40
    territory, *141*
    and young wolves, 52
Paiute people, 27
Paquet, Paul, 56
Pasteur, Louis, 84
Pawnee people,
    legends, 21, 29, 31, 32, 29
    warriors, 93, 102, 104
pendants, *142*
People of the Sacred Mountain, 99
Perrault, Charles, 129
Peters, Roger, *125*

Peterson, Rolf O., 77
physical characteristics,
    of *Canis* species, 168, 169
    of wolves (*Canis lupus*), 168
pitfalls (deadfalls), 135, 137
Plautus, 87
play, 46, *47*
Plenty Coups, 112
Pliny the Elder, 116
Plutarch, 119
poaching, 159
Point Barrow, Alaska, *27*
Poland, 142
Ponca people, 102
population,
    of Canis species, 168, 169
    of wolves (*Canis lupus*), 136,
        144, 154, 155, 156, 158, 164,
        168
Portugal, 140, 168
predation. *See* hunting
prey, 40, 69, 77, 79, 80, 138. *See*
    also hunting
Prussia, 138
Pueblo people, 27
pups (cubs), *38*, 40, 45–46, *47*, 49

Quillayute ritual, 60

rabies, 84, 116
range,
    of *Canis* species, 168, 169
    of wolves (*Canis lupus*), 154, 168
Rasmussen, Knud, 137
rattle, *61*
red dog. *See* dhole
Red Riding Hood, 13, *14*, 125, 129
Red Wing, 98
red wolves (*Canis rufus*), 22, 25,
    168–69
Rehnmark, Eva, 82
Reid, Bill, *142*
Reindeer Chukchee shaman, 113
reintroducing wolves, 153, 154, 162
relationships,
    hierarchies, 39, 40, 51, 75
    with humans, 57–59
    pack, 39–62
    with prey, 80
rendezvous sites, 49
Remus. *See* Romulus and Remus.
Report No. 35, 156
rituals, 60–61, 93–119, 136
    Native North American,
        60–61, 98–105, 112–16, 119
    shamans, 101–102, 112–16, 119
    Viking, 94–95

wolf societies, 60–61,
    104–105
Rocky Mountains, 161
Romania, 140, 146
Romulus and Remus, 59, 60, 118,
    119
Russia, 146, 154, 156

Saami people, 156
Sarsi (Tsuu T'ina) people, *104*, 137
Saxo Grammaticus, 95
Scandinavian legends, 28
scent glands, 51
scent-marking, 39, 51
Schleidt, Wolfgang M., *84*, 128
Scotland, 101, 138
Seton, Ernest Thompson, 44, 51
Sextus Placitus, 116
sexual maturity, 42
Shakespeare, William, 118
Shalter, Michael D., *84*
"Shaman-as-Wolf," 114
Shamanism in North America, 114
shamans, 101–102, 112–16, 119, 137
Shoshone people, 27
Siberian Yakut shaman, 112
Sicily, Italy, 116
Siegfried, 59
Simien jackals (*Canis simensis*),
    22, 169
Sioux people, 103, 105
Sirius, 21, 29, *33*
Sitting Bull, *102*, 103
size,
    of *Canis* species, 168, 169
    of wolves (*Canis lupus*), 45, 49,
        168
Skidi (Skiri) Pawnee people, 31, 32,
    98, 99
skins, 105, 112, 144, 146
Skinwalker, 116
Sköll, 28
smell, 51
Smietana, Wojciech, 155
Smith, Doug, 162
Soul of the Wolf, The, 158
Soviet Union (former), 154, 155
Spain, 101, 140, 158, 168
speed, *145*
Spengler, Oswald, 155
sport, shooting wolves for, 146
status,
    of *Canis* species, 168, 169
    of wolves (*Canis lupus*), 168
Stefansson, Vilhjalmur, 82
Steinhart, Peter, *153*, *159*
Sturluson, Snorri, 94, 96

submission, 39, 51
subspecies of *Canis*, 22, 168–69
supernatural powers, 93, 98, 104–
    105, 112–16
superstitions, 118, 119
Sutton Hoo, England, *105*
Sweden, *94*, 156
Sword, 104

teeth, 116
territory, 52, *141*
Theberge, John B., *39*, 54
timeline, of wolf control, 138
tipi, *104*
Tirawa the Great Creator, 32
Tlingit art, *99*, *137*
Tluukwaana, 60
Tokawa people, 27
Torslunda, Sweden, *94*
trapping, 126, 144
Tseshatiake, 103
Tsimshian (Gitksan) wolf
    headdress, *118*
Tsistsistas (Cheyenne) people,
    66, 98
Turkish legends, 40, 58

ulfhednar, *94*, 95
ungulates, 143
United States Fish and Wildlife
    Service (USFWS), 161, 164
United States, 140, 143–44,
    146, 154, 160–62, 164. *See
    also names of individual
    locations*
urine, 51, 52
Ut'set, 27
Utah, 161
Uttar Pradesh, India, 84

Vargas Island, Canada, 84
Vikings, 93, *94*–96, 98, 105
Vivarais, France, 84
Völuspa, 96

Wales, 84, 138
warriors, 93–119
    Middle Ages, 94
    Native, 98–105, 112–16
    Vikings, 94–96, 98
Washington, 161
weight,
    of *Canis* species, 168, 169
    of wolves (*Canis lupus*), 168
werewolves, 125, 130, 133, 134
"White American Wolf," *81*

White Wolf (legendary character),
    29
white wolves, *12*
Wilson, P. J., 25
Wisagatcak the Trickster, 26
Wisconsin, 143, 154
Wissler, Clark, 101
witches, 115, 116
Wolf (legendary character), 27
wolf-Apollo, 28
"Wolf-as-Shaman," 114
Wolf Bundle, 31
Wolf Dance, *61*
Wolf Dancer, *40*
Wolf in North American History,
    122
"wolf in sheep's clothing," 129
wolf-killers, baleen, 135
Wolf-Man (Arikara legend), 27
Wolf Man, The (1941), *133*
Wolf People. *See* Pawnee people
Wolf Reclassification Rule, 161
*Wolf Ritual of the Northwest
    Coast, The*, 60
Wolf Road (Milky Way), 29
wolfskins, 105, 112, 144, 146
wolf societies (human), 60–61, 93,
    103, 104–105
Wolf Star (legendary character),
    32
Wolf Star (Sirius), 21, 29, 31, *33*
Wolves of Isle Royale, The, 77
Wood Buffalo National Park,
    Canada, 80
Wyoming, 140, 154, 162

Yakut (Sakha) shaman, 112
Yellowstone National Park, 138,
    160, 161, 162
Ynglinga Saga, 95
Yokuts people, 27
young wolves, 52
Young, Stanley Paul, 122
Yukon, Canada, 143

Zuni Beast God, 119